WELSH NATIONAL OPERA

GRAFFEG

Published by Graffeg
First Published Spring 2006
Copyright © Graffeg 2006
ISBN-13: 978 1 905582 00 6
ISBN-10: 1 905582 00 5

Graffeg Limited
Radnor Court
256 Cowbridge Road East,
Cardiff CF5 1GZ Wales UK
Tel: +44(0)29 2037 7312
sales@graffeg.com
www.graffeg.com
are hereby identified as the authors of
this work in accordance with section
77 of the Copyrights, Designs and
Patents Act 1988

Distributed by the Welsh Books Council
www.cllc.org.uk
castellbrychan@clc.org.uk

A CIP Catalogue record for this book is
available from the British Library

Designed and produced by
Peter Gill & Associates
sales@petergill.com
www.petergill.com

Cover Photograph: *Ariadne auf Naxos*
2004 Janice Watson as Ariadne and
Peter Hoare as Bacchus
Photograph Clive Barda.

**Welsh National Opera –
Celebrating the first 60 years**
Edited by Caroline Leech

Thanks to the following:
Peter Gill & Associates for designing
the book, Art direction Peter Gill,
Designers Kelly Walters and
Carwyn Lloyd Jones

The publishers are also grateful to the
Welsh Books Council for their support
and marketing advice.
www.cllc.org.uk

WELSH
NATIONAL
OPERA

This book is dedicated to everyone who has made Welsh National Opera the world-class company it is today.

Cyflwynir y llyfr hwn i bawb sydd wedi helpu gwneud Opera Cenedlaethol Cymru yn gwmni o safon fyd-eang, fel y mae heddiw.

Over the last 60 years, Welsh National Opera has grown from a group of passionate amateur music-makers into one of the world's great opera companies.

As the curtain rose on their first performance in 1946, did any of those pioneers realize the true significance of what they were starting? Perhaps not, but in their hearts was a belief that they were giving people in Wales the chance to see and hear outstanding opera, probably for the first time. Much has changed in WNO over the last six decades, but the Company retains at its core that deep passion for producing exceptional operas and the strong commitment to take them to audiences across Wales, the UK and far beyond.

I hope that as you read this book, and enjoy the photographic reminders of WNO's excellent productions, you will have a sense of what WNO was, is now, and will be in years to come.

As its proud Patron, and very nearly the same age myself, I wish Welsh National Opera a very happy 60th birthday, and I think we can all expect the next sixty years to be even more outstanding than the last.

Yn ystod y chwe deg mlynedd diwethaf, mae Opera Cenedlaethol Cymru wedi tyfu o fod yn grŵp o gerddorion amatur angerddol i fod yn un o gwmnïau opera mawr y byd.

Pan gododd y llenni ar eu perfformiad cyntaf ym 1946, a oedd unrhyw un ymhlith yr arloeswyr hynny'n sylweddoli gwir arwyddocâd yr hyn roedden nhw'n ei gychwyn? Hwyrach nad oeddent, ond yn eu calonnau roedden nhw'n argyhoeddedig eu bod yn rhoi i bobl Cymru y cyfle i weld a chlywed operâu godidog, a hynny am y tro cyntaf, efallai. Mae llawer wedi newid yn OCC yn ystod y trigain mlynedd diwethaf, ond craidd y Cwmni o hyd yw'r dyhead dwfn am gynhyrchu operâu eithriadol a'r ymrwymiad cadarn i'w cyflwyno i gynulleidfaoedd ar hyd a lled Cymru, y Deyrnas Gyfunol a thu hwnt.

Gobeithio, wrth i chi ddarllen y llyfr hwn, a mwynhau'r darluniau i'n hatgoffa o gynyrchiadau rhagorol OCC, y cewch syniad o'r hyn oedd OCC, yr hyn ydyw nawr ac a fydd yn y blynyddoedd i ddod.

Fel ei Noddwr balch, a bron yr un oed fy hun, rwyf yn dymuno pen-blwydd hapus iawn i Opera Cenedlaethol Cymru. Rwy'n credu y gallwn i gyd ddisgwyl i'r trigain mlynedd nesaf fod hyd yn oed yn fwy eithriadol na'r trigain mlynedd cyntaf.

A welcome from Carlo Rizzi, Music Director, Welsh National Opera
Croeso gan Carlo Rizzi, Cyfarwyddwr Cerdd, Opera Cenedlaethol Cymru

Welsh National Opera is 60 years old! A birthday like this is a great time to look back at all our achievements over six decades, and to look forward to the years to come with excitement and ambition.

It all began in humble surroundings with a group of clerks, shopkeepers and miners. By the time the Company reached 30, it had turned professional, and not long ago it moved into its first home, Wales Millennium Centre in Cardiff Bay. Undoubtedly there were low times when funding was scarce or hard-fought battles were lost, but in recompense there have been many, many more breathtaking highs.

In his book, which was published in 1986 charting the history of the first 40 years of WNO, Richard Fawkes signed off with: 'it is, as it always has been, a company that makes one expect miracles.' Those first four miraculous decades gave us a solid bedrock on which to keep building

the artistic quality, the reputation and the reach of Welsh National Opera's work.

This book remembers those early decades with thanks, and takes the story on beyond Richard's book. As a photographic celebration of the last twenty years in particular, it tries to capture in still life the heat, the colour, the energy and the passion of some of WNO's greatest productions. It will also give you some insight into the people and the places behind the scenes that make it happen.

I hope that your journey through this book will evoke special memories if you saw these productions, and will entice and captivate you if you didn't. Above all, I hope it will give you even further reason to join us on our journey into the next 60 years.

Mae Opera Cenedlaethol Cymru yn 60 oed! Mae pen-blwydd fel hwn yn amser da i edrych yn ôl ar ein holl lwyddiannau dros dri degawd, ac i edrych ymlaen at y blynyddoedd i ddod gyda chyffro ac uchelgais.

Dechreuwyd y cyfan yn ddigon distadl gan grŵp o glercod, siopwyr a glowyr. Erbyn iddo gyrraedd ei 30 oed, roedd y Cwmni wedi troi'n gwmni proffesiynol, ac yn ddiweddar iawn symudodd i'w gartref cyntaf yng Nghanolfan Mileniwm Cymru ym Mae Caerdydd. Yn sicr, cafwyd adegau anodd pan oedd yr arian yn

brin neu pan gollwyd brwydrau caled. Ond i wneud iawn am hynny, cafwyd nifer fawr, fawr o uchafbwyntiau llawer mwy gogoneddus.

Yn y llyfr hwn, a gyhoeddwyd ym 1986 i ddilyn hanes 40 mlynedd cyntaf OCC, roedd Richard Fawkes yn gorffen drwy ddweud 'mae'n gwmni sydd nawr, fel erioed, yn gwneud i chi ddisgwyl gwyrthiau.' Roedd y deugain mlynedd cyntaf gwyrthiol hynny yn sail gadarn i ni ddal i adeiladu ar safon artistig, enw gwych a chyrhaeddiad Opera Cenedlaethol Cymru.

Mae'r llyfr hwn yn cofio'r degawdau cynnar hynny gyda diolchgarwch, ac mae'n parhau'r hanes ar ôl cyhoeddi llyfr Richard. Fel dathliad o'r ugain mlynedd diwethaf yn benodol, drwy gyfrwng lluniau, mae'n ceisio cyfleu drwy luniau llonydd y gwres, y lliw, yr egni a'r angerdd yn rhai o operâu mwyaf arbennig OCC. Bydd hefyd yn rhoi cipolwg i chi ar y bobl a'r mannau y tu ôl i'r llenni sy'n gwneud i'r cyfan ddigwydd.

Gobeithio y bydd eich siwrnai drwy'r llyfr hwn yn dod at atgofion arbennig os gwelsoch y cynyrchiadau, ac yn eich denu a'ch swyno os na welsoch nhw. Yn anad dim, gobeithio y bydd yn rheswm pellach eto i chi ymuno â ni ar ein siwrnai drwy'r 60 mlynedd nesaf.

Photograph/Llun Clive Barda

Contents

1945

			Arrears	Jan 4	11	18	Feb 1	8	15	22	Mar 1	8	15	Apr 5	12	19
	ASH-CHILDS.	PHYLLIS.	-	-	1/-	-	-	-	2/-	-	1/-	6	6	6	6
	HOWELLS	J.T.													
	BRIDGEWATER.	A.M.	6	-	1/6	-	-	-	2/-	-	1/-	6	6	6	6
	BAKER.	CHARLES.	20/6	-	-	-	-	-	-	-	-	-	-	-	-
	BOWEN.	1	4	-	2/-	-	1/6	-	1/-	-	1/-	-	-	-	2/-
	BARNES.	JOAN.	6	1/-	6	-	-	1/6	6	6	-	1/-	6	6	6
	JAMES.	FRANK.													
	CHALLINOR.	RALPH.	11/-	-	-	-	-	-	-	-	-	-	-	-	-
(EDDINS)	CREASE.	JOY.	6	1/-	6	6	-	1/-	-	1/6	6	6	6	6	6
	COOK.	E.C.	3/-	-	-	-	-	-	-	7/-	6	6	-	1/-	-
July 28	COURT.	TOM.	-	6	-	6	-	1/-	6	6	6	6	6	6	6	6
	CLEMENT.	E.													
	DAVIES.	ELSIE	-	-	-	-	-	2/6	6	-	-	-	2/-	-	1/-
	DAVIES	GEOFF	-	-	-	1/6	-	-	-	6	1/-	1/-	1/-	-	1/-
	DAVIES	A.G.	-	-	1/-	-	-	-	2/-	6	-	-	-	2/6
	DUDDERIDGE.	Wm.	6	-	-	-	-	6	6	6	6	6	6	6	-
	FERRIS.	W.J												6
	EVANS.	NELLIE	-	-	-	1/6	-	1/-	6	-	-	-	-	3/-
	EVANS.	FRANK.	-	-	-	1/6	-	1/-	6	-	-	-	-	3/-
	EVANS.	LILIAN	-	-	1/-	-	-	2/-	✓	-	1/-	1/-	✓	-	-
	EVANS	DAVID	1/6	-	-	-	-	-	2/-	-	-	-	2/6	-	2/-
	EASTERBROOK.	AUDREY.	-	-	-	2/-	✓	6	1/-	✓	6	-	2/-	✓	✓
	EVANS.	RONALD.	1/6	2/-	-	-	-	-	-	-	-	-	-	-
	GOUGH.	BEATRICE	-	6	6	6	-	1/-	6	6	6	6	6	-	1/-
	GRIFFITHS.	MARG.	6	1/-	6	6	-	1/-	6	6	6	6	6	6	6
Aug 1	GITTINS	W.	-	-	-	1/6	-	1/-	6	6	-	1/-	6	6	6
Aug 13	GRIFFITHS.	ENA.	-	6	-	1/-	-	1/-	6	-	1/-	6	6	-	1/-	6
	HAWKINS	KAY.	-	-	1/-	6	-	1/6	6	-	1/-	6	-	-	1/6
	HAZELL.	ETHEL.	-	-	1/-	-	-	-	2/-	-	-	-	-	1/6
	HAZELL.	W.H.	-	-	1/-	-	-	-	2/-	-	-	1/6	-	-	1/6	-

8

The first 40 years

In 1985 **Richard Fawkes** wrote *Welsh National Opera*, a book which charted in detail the 40 years of WNO. Twenty years on, Richard has revisited his book and remembers here the pioneers of WNO – the coalminers, nurses and shopkeepers who strove to give opera to Wales and beyond. Forty years of ground-breaking work firmly laid the foundation for WNO at the heart of Welsh cultural life, developing it into the world-class company it is today.

From 1945 onwards the members of Welsh National Opera Company would pay 6d to attend each rehearsal, and a log was kept of their attendance and timely payment of subs.

1943 – 1952

1943 2 December

The Welsh National Opera Company was formed; 28 people signed up to join.

1946 15 April

The first ever performance by the Welsh National Opera Company at the Prince of Wales Theatre, Cardiff – the double-bill of *Cavalleria rusticana* and *I Pagliacci*.

1949 21 November

The first opera performance in Swansea – *The Bartered Bride* - featuring the Swansea section of the Voluntary Chorus.

The opening performances of *Cavalleria rusticana* and *I Pagliacci* were very much a team effort, with singers sewing costumes and painting sets right up to opening night.

They came from all over South Wales: miners, doctors, teachers, secretaries, shop assistants, solicitors, steel workers, housewives. Many couldn't read music but all were united in their passion for singing and desperate to join the chorus of a new opera company being formed in Cardiff by Idloes Owen. Owen, a former miner turned singing teacher (whose best-known pupil was Geraint Evans), dreamed of forming a company that would play the major Welsh towns, with leading roles taken by Welsh singers, who were then having to go to London to find fame and fortune, and amateur choruses drawn locally.

The new Welsh National Opera (no one remembers who gave it this name rather than the planned Lyrian Grand Opera Company) opened at the Prince of Wales Theatre in Cardiff on 15 April 1946 with a double-bill of *Cavalleria rusticana*, conducted by Owen, and *I Pagliacci*, conducted by Ivor John from

Swansea. The following night *Faust* was given, with John again the conductor. All three operas were performed in hired sets and costumes.

Few if any who took part in those sell-out performances could have realised just what they were starting. One person who did was garage owner Bill Smith. A former secretary of the defunct Cardiff Grand Opera and supernumerary on British National Opera tours to Cardiff, Smith had been to opera houses in Italy after the First World War and longed to create something similar in Wales. Invited by Idloes Owen to run the business side of the new company, he soon recognised the potential. A piano was moved into his first floor Frederick Street showroom and once a week the cars were pushed to one side to create a rehearsal space. He took producer Norman Jones on to the garage staff so he could concentrate on producing.

1951 September

1952 7 October

The first opera tour to North and Mid-Wales, with seasons in Llandudno and Aberystwyth.

The première of Verdi's Nabucco, WNO's first in-house production and the first time the opera had been staged in the UK in over a century.

As performances approached, a section of the showroom was curtained off to store costumes and props. Smith spent much of his time in London talking to people at Covent Garden and Sadler's Wells about rising stars, and he became legendary for attracting young talent for small fees. When looking for a conductor to take charge of *The Tales of Hoffman* in 1950, he was told about a young Australian repetiteur at Sadler's Wells who wanted to make a name for himself. Smith promptly booked him. The young man was Charles Mackerras.

Determined that WNO would eventually stand comparison with any other opera company in the world, Smith was always on the lookout for people who could help raise standards. In 1952 he was approached by producer John Moody to stage Verdi's *Nabucco*. With its Biblical story, its subtext of a captive nation longing for freedom, and its need for

a superb chorus, Verdi's third opera was ideal for WNO, and Smith decided it should be the Company's first in-house production.

This was a massive undertaking for what was still in many ways a typical amateur company. Seven sets were needed; every member of the eighty-strong chorus required two costumes; footwear had to be found, beards made and props constructed. A couple of cottages close to Smith's garage were taken over to become the wardrobe. Space for building the sets was found above the coffee business run by the stage manager. Everyone who could wield a needle mucked in, including Bill Smith's wife. Ten minutes before she was due on stage as Abigaille on opening night, Soprano Ruth Packer was still sewing rings onto the temple curtains.

Nabucco had not been staged in Britain for over a hundred years and attracted the London critics to the Sophia Gardens Pavilion

From its early days, WNO was able to attract some of the world's best opera singers, and indeed gave many young singers their first steps to international renown. Elizabeth Vaughan, Dame Gwyneth Jones, Sir Geraint Evans and Elisabeth Söderström (overleaf) all sang with WNO. Photographs Julian Shepherd

1953 – 1969

The first WNO performances outside Wales opened at the Bournemouth Pavilion with *Nabucco*.

WNO's first performance at the New Theatre in Cardiff at which it would perform for the next 50 years.

The first WNO London Season opened at Sadler's Wells with *Mefistofele*.

The Chorus of WNO in *A Midsummer Marriage*
Photograph
Julian Shepherd

(the Prince of Wales Theatre had meanwhile become a cinema showing sex films). Expecting some worthy amateur operation, they were astonished by the high standard, especially of the chorus. The operatic world suddenly took notice of what was happening in Wales.

The Chorus was very much the jewel in WNO's crown and repertoire was invariably chosen with them in mind. As well as the more popular operas, early Verdi works such as *Sicilian Vespers*, *I lombardi* and *La battaglia di Legnano*, none of which had been seen in Britain for a very long time were staged. So too was Rimsky-Korsakov's equally rare *May Night*. However the plan to recruit choruses throughout Wales never happened. Besides the chorus in Cardiff, the only other to be formed was in Swansea. There was intense rivalry between the two. The Swansea chorus may have been smaller in number than

its Cardiff counterpart but it more than made up for in volume. The Chorus also caused a permanent headache to the producer for, no matter where he put it, there was a gaggle of women (known in Cardiff as the Swansea Witches) who would always sneak their way to the front.

Without a permanent home (the New Theatre had become the company's Cardiff base in 1954), WNO had to tour to survive, and that meant not just touring in Wales (on what were described in Arts Council documents as 'missionary tours') but over the border into England. As the number of weeks on the road increased, organising such tours – with an amateur chorus whose members did not know if they could get time off work – became an administrative nightmare. When the company played Llandudno for the first time (following a circus, which meant that everyone had to scrub out backstage to remove the smell of

The first rehearsal of the 30 members of the new professional Chorus, The WNO Chorale, becoming The Chorus of WNO in 1979.

WNO moved into its new John Street headquarters, with the neighbouring Princess of Wales building being opened in 1984.

the animals) or travelled by special train to appear in Bournemouth, most of the chorus had to take their summer holidays to be there. When the company made its first London appearance at Sadler's Wells in July 1955 (in the middle of a heatwave), mezzo Muriel Pointon, who ran a butcher's shop in Cardiff, had to work in the shop every morning, catch the midday train to London, perform, then catch the overnight train back to Cardiff and go straight to the market to buy meat. She did not sleep once in a bed that week.

As tour dates approached, choristers also found that they were being asked to rehearse five nights a week. To achieve his goal of a fully professional company that could attract opera lovers from around the world, Smith knew that the amateur chorus had to be dropped. It was not an easy decision to take and it produced considerable resentment

among those who felt the company had been taken out of the hands of people for whom it had been started. Nevertheless in 1968 a thirty-strong professional Chorale was formed. Ten amateurs decided to throw in their day jobs and join; these included Gordon Whyte, a former steelworker in the bass section. He later recalled that the only difference after they turned professional was they no longer sang on the bus.

But the amateurs were not out of it completely. The Voluntary Chorus, as they became known, still supplemented the Chorale in the big choral operas. When distinguished bass Richard Van Allan first sang Zaccaria in *Nabucco* with the company, there was no prior dress rehearsal because everyone knew the production so well. Van Allan rehearsed only with the Chorale, and was merely warned that on the night the stage would be a little more crowded by the added presence of some

WNO has been able to attract a loyal audience in every theatre to which it tours.
Photographs
Julian Shepherd

1970 – 1986

1970 August

1973 June

1973 14 December

First performance by WNO's own orchestra; originally The Welsh Philharmonia, it became The Orchestra of WNO in 1979.

WNO's first foreign tour – performing *Billy Budd* in Lausanne and Zurich, in Switzerland.

The final performance of the WNO Voluntary Chorus after 40 years of work.

Forbes Robinson as Claggart in *Billy Budd* which took WNO on its first foreign tour in 1973. WNO formed its own Orchestra in 1970.
Photographs Julian Shepherd

seventy amateurs. Pushing his way through this crowd on opening night, he was about to sing his first line when he felt a tug on his sleeve from an agitated member of the Voluntary Chorus. 'I stand there,' the man said; 'been standing there for years.' 'Well you're not standing here tonight,' hissed Van Allan, turning to deliver his opening line.

Van Allan was just one of many young artists given their first chance of a leading role by WNO. Never having had resources of some other opera companies, WNO has always had to survive by attracting young talent before they became too expensive. Among famous names given their first opportunities by WNO schoolteacher Stuart Burrows; Gwyneth Jones; Margaret Price and Delme Bryn-Jones. From further afield came Glyndebourne chorister Josephine Barstow, whose appearances as Violetta brought London critics who agreed she was a talent and would go far. Then there

was Thomas Allen, a young graduate of the Royal College who had been coached there by WNO's musical director James Lockhart. Allen made his professional debut in a school hall in Haverfordwest, singing Baron Douphol in *La traviata*.

Lockart was succeeded by his 30 year old assistant, Richard Armstrong. In 1973 the company made its first overseas visit and the Voluntary Chorus was disbanded. 166 musicians, singers and backstage crew flew from Cardiff to Switzerland to give three performances of *Billy Budd*. Two days earlier the set – all eight tons of it – had left by road. Terence Sharpe sang the role of Billy in two performances in Lausanne; Thomas Allen, who was singing Papageno at Glyndebourne, flew in to give the single performance in Zurich. It was Lockhart's final appearance as music director and he went out in a blaze of glory on an emotion-charged evening.

1984

Cardiff Theatrical Services was created from WNO's workshops to build sets for WNO as well as for many other opera companies.

1986 Autumn

WNO celebrated its 40th birthday with Wagner's *Ring Cycle*, the first time it was produced by a regional opera company in the UK.

Touring to Swansea and Llandudno, and further afield to Manchester, Southampton, Birmingham, Peterborough, Sunderland and other English cities, made the logistics of getting the Voluntary Chorus to the various venues very hit-or-miss. It was never known how many would turn up. In Liverpool, the bus arrived with only one bass on board. In Sunderland, a member of the Voluntary Chorus in *Aida*, who was supposed to lead in an army, was followed on by a single soldier. The Voluntary Chorus had outlived its usefulness, and made its final appearance in a performance of *Don Carlos* in Southampton in December 1973.

On stage with them for her only stage appearance, dressed in costume but promising not to sing, was Margaret Moreland, WNO's company secretary. No account of WNO, however brief, would be complete without mention of the remarkable Peggy Moreland.

She had just given up her job in a solicitor's office in order to spend more time at home with her family when she was invited into Frederick Street in 1949 by Bill Smith to help out for a couple of days to type the minutes of a board meeting. She left thirty-seven years later. If Smith was the general, Moreland was the lieutenant. He had the ideas; she made them happen.

Over the years, WNO had worked with a number of orchestras, including the scratch orchestras of the early days; the Bournemouth Symphony (which first brought their conductor and later WNO Music Director Charles Groves to the company); Liverpool Philharmonic; CBSO, and Sinfonia of Wales. Finally the go-ahead was given for the company to form their own. Initially called the Welsh Philharmonia, as it was expected to be giving concerts when it was not in the pit, its membership was largely drawn from

Serban's *Eugene Onegin* in 1980.
Photograph
Julian Shepherd
The Rhinegold from WNO's *Ring Cycle*, performed in full in 1986.
Photograph
Clive Barda

1995 – 2006

1995 December

The application for Lottery funding for the Cardiff Bay Opera House was refused by the Millennium Commission.

2001

WNO MAX's first project, the RPS Award-winning *Katerina*, was premièred in Merthyr Tydfil with over 200 local children taking part.

2002 February

The Arts Councils of England and Wales announced a £4.25 million Stabilisation Award to WNO to give it a firmer financial base from which to work.

Bryn Terfel's first *Marriage of Figaro* in 1990, with Julie Gossage as Cherubino.
Photograph Brian Tarr

WNO MAX's award-winning *Katerina*.
Photograph Barry Hamilton

London-based musicians and the orchestra's first rehearsal took place in St Pancras Town Hall. In charge of them was a young American who had been brought in by Lockhart to conduct *Aida* and *The Barber of Seville*. Later to become Music Director of The Met, James Levine made his British operatic debut conducting *Aida* in Llandudno.

By the time Brian McMaster became General Administrator in 1976, WNO was a fully professional company with a 48-strong professional chorus and its own orchestra. Shortly after McMaster's appointment, the scenery dock in Cardiff caught fire, and all the sets from the previous thirty years either went up in smoke or were so badly damaged that they were unusable. Other companies rallied round and the season went ahead in a series of makeshift sets. McMaster's great contribution was to bring in directors from the straight theatre and the Eastern European tradition. Not everyone liked the results, but Harry Kupfer's production of *Elektra* (1978) became a major landmark in modern opera production. There was also Järvefelt's *The Magic Flute*, Stein's *Otello* and Herz's *Madam Butterfly*. Even Ruth Berghaus's *Don Giovanni*, which divided the critics, brought a theatrical magic to opera production that had not been seen in Britain before.

Another important person brought in at this time was Reginald Goodall. At 78 Reggie, as he was always known, was considered by many to be the greatest Wagnerian conductor of his generation, even though his talents had not always been recognised at the Royal Opera House. In 1979, McMaster invited him to conduct his first *Tristan und Isolde*. When he arrived in Cardiff to begin rehearsals, Reggie climbed onto the podium while McMaster made a speech of welcome. The orchestra sat, waiting for him to say a

WNO celebrated its first performance in its new home in Wales Millennium Centre – *La traviata* and *Wozzeck*.

WNO's 60th birthday marked with a performance of *The Flying Dutchman* at the Grand Theatre, Swansea.

few words. Instead he looked at his score and began turning pages. After a while, he looked up. 'Gentlemen,' he said, 'I have begun.'

During McMaster's tenure, the name of the Chorale was changed to the Chorus of WNO. McMaster asked the choristers which name they wanted: 'Chorale' or 'Chorus of WNO'. The decision was unanimous that they should stay as the Chorale. The next day McMaster put up a notice announcing that henceforth they would be known as the Chorus of WNO. Why did McMaster ignore their wishes? He later said, that is was because they were wrong.

While never ignoring the popular repertoire – including coming up with such striking productions as Lucian Pintilie's *Carmen*, set in a circus ring – WNO continued to explore interesting and unusual repertoire. Berg's *Lulu* had been given its first British

staging as was Martinů's *The Greek Passion*. Handel's *Rodelinda* was performed at a time when most Handel operas were not considered to be stageable. There was a surge of interest in Janáček thanks to the co-productions with Scottish Opera. Even the operatic peaks of a *Ring Cycle* were scaled under the baton of Richard Armstrong.

Forty years after it first took to the stage as an enthusiastic amateur company, Welsh National Opera was rightly being hailed as the most inventive, most imaginative and most adventurous of all the British opera companies.

WNO's new home, Wales Millennium Centre which lies at the heart of the regeneration of the Cardiff Bay area. Photograph Peter Gill

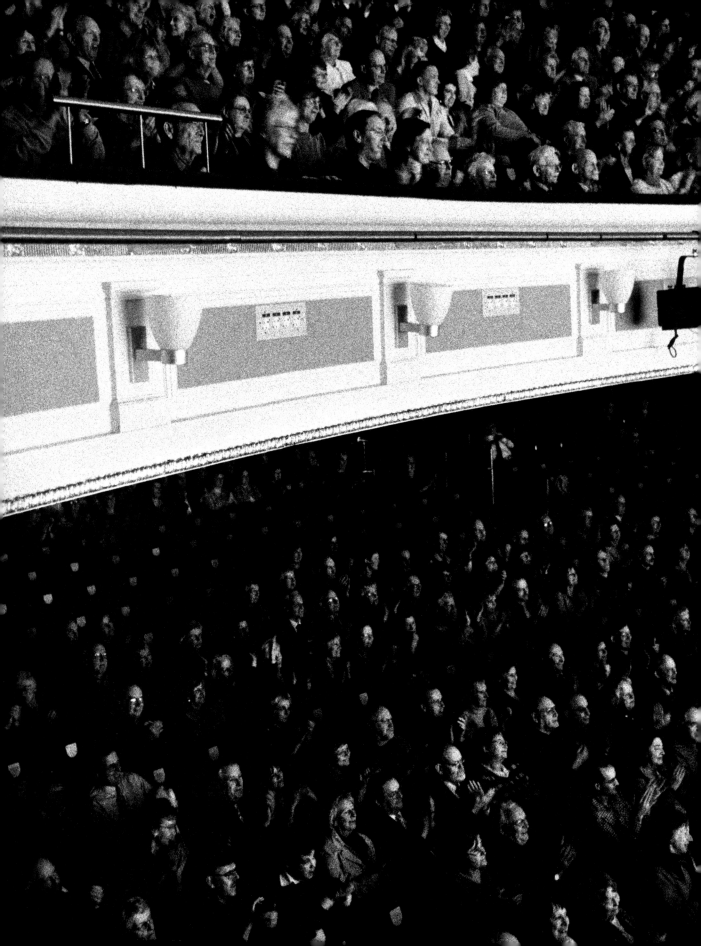

WNO is the UK's largest touring opera company, reaching almost 140,000 people in cities across the UK each year. Until 2004 and the opening of Wales Millennium Centre, WNO opened each season at the New Theatre in Cardiff before taking to the road. With his camera, documentary photographer **Kiran Ridley** stalked the WNO Company during a New Theatre season, and joined them on tour to the Birmingham Hippodrome. Kiran offers a rare insight into WNO's life on the road.

Reaching musical maturity

During 30 years as a fully professional company, WNO has continued to develop the quality of its productions and its music, and to earn its status as a world-class company. **Simon Rees**, WNO's Dramaturg, talked to WNO's three General Directors about the musical development of the Company during that time. In particular he sought their insight into the influence of WNO's Music Directors - Sir Richard Armstrong, Sir Charles Mackerras, Carlo Rizzi and Tugan Sokhiev.

The Orchestra and Chorus of WNO rehearsing in Orchestra Hall at WNO's former headquarters in John Street.
Photograph Brian Tarr

The collaborative role between General Director and Music Director has always been at the heart of Welsh National Opera's principles and practice as a company. Sir Brian McMaster, WNO's General Administrator (later Managing Director) from 1976 to 1991, when he became Director of the Edinburgh International Festival explains:

'I believe that the relationship between a general director and a musical director should be unbelievably close – like a marriage, in a way – so that each saves the other from their worst failings.'

When Brian McMaster arrived at WNO, Richard Armstrong had been Musical Director since 1973; he had been Assistant Musical Director to James Lockhart since 1968, and had made his conducting debut there with *The Marriage of Figaro* in 1969. The partnership between McMaster and Armstrong resulted in some

of the Company's most ambitious productions to date, including Wagner's *Ring Cycle*, directed by Göran Järvefelt, which opened in 1983 with *The Rhinegold*. It was not the most obvious choice for the Company, as Brian McMaster recollects:

'We both decided that the one thing we wouldn't do was the *Ring Cycle*. But then when Järvefelt directed *The Magic Flute* I said to Richard: "I think we've found somebody who would do a Ring." Nicholas Payne [then Financial Controller] was there too, and we had a discussion. I thought we had found the way to do it. As we talked, the cast fell into our mind, and we did it.'

When asked whether this had not seemed at the time to absurdly and ambitiously stretch the Company's resources, Brian McMaster responded:

'I think every step we took did: *Elektra*, *Die Frau ohne Schatten*, the Stein *Otello* and *Falstaff*, and *The Trojans*. But that's the whole point, you push the boundaries on a continual basis.'

Richard Armstrong left WNO in 1986 to become Principal Guest Conductor at Frankfurt Opera, and later became Music Director of Scottish Opera, a post he held until 2005, the year in which he received a knighthood. Sir Charles Mackerras succeeded him as Musical Director in 1987, and held the post until 1992.

Charles Mackerras first conducted at WNO in the Company's earliest years, when in 1950 he conducted *The Tales of Hoffmann*, *The Bartered Bride* and *Die Fledermaus*. Between then and his appointment as Musical Director, he conducted the Company for only three productions. The last of these, in 1984, was the controversial production of *Don Giovanni* by

'I believe that the relationship between a general director and a musical director should be unbelievably close – like a marriage, in a way – so that each saves the other from their worst failings.' Sir Brian McMaster

Sir Richard Armstrong
Photograph Clive Barda

Sir Charles Mackerras
Photograph Clive Barda

'It was a great time. I think we were very lucky to have a conductor of that quality as Musical Director, firming a relationship with the Company which still exists very strongly today.' Sir Brian McMaster

Ruth Berghaus, about which Mackerras has subsequently spoken critically. Brian McMaster, recalls, however, that at the time:

'There were odd moments during the rehearsal period, but Charles had huge respect for Ruth Berghaus because she directed from the full score: she was 110% musical. When Charles conducted the performances, it was Berghaus's *Don Giovanni* production that he conducted. He was completely integrated with it, and made something amazing of it.'

Sir Charles Mackerras's appointment as Music Director came out of that production. He brought to WNO his deep experience as conductor and musicologist, as well as his administrative experience as Chief Conductor at the Hamburg State Opera, and as Music Director of Sadler's Wells Opera, which during his period of tenure, from 1970-77 became English National Opera. At WNO, both as Musical Director and later as Conductor Emeritus, he brought his experience to performances of Mozart, Strauss, Sullivan and his great subject of expertise, Janáček, as well as to great and memorable performances of *Tristan und Isolde*. Brian McMaster recalls:
'It was a great time. I think we were very lucky to have a conductor of that quality as Musical Director,

firming a relationship with the Company which still exists very strongly today.'

Although it was Brian McMaster who appointed Carlo Rizzi as Musical Director to succeed Sir Charles Mackerras, Rizzi began his first period of office (1992-2002) under Matthew Epstein, WNO's next General Director. Matthew Epstein had been associated with WNO during his years as a jury member of the BBC Cardiff Singer of the World competition. As a manager of the New York artists' management company, Columbia Artists Management, he had also been involved in WNO's work with singers represented by that organisation. Matthew had been a friend of Brian McMaster since the early 70s, and had brought many young American artists to his attention, often from other artist management firms. Since 1980 he had also been artistic adviser to the Lyric Opera, Chicago, and had acted as a consultant to several other companies, including the Kennedy Center, Santa Fe Opera, Netherlands Opera and San Francisco Opera. From 1987 to 1990 he was Artistic Director of Opera at the Brooklyn Academy of Music, where he hosted WNO's first American visit with a presentation of the Stein production of *Falstaff*. Matthew Epstein's

love of singing, and his range of international connections, allowed his period of tenure to broaden the Company's scope in drawing conductors, directors and singers from around the world.

'During my stay at WNO, there were two Musical Directors. I was lucky enough to have Sir Charles Mackerras's last season at WNO and Carlo Rizzi's first season. By the time I got to Wales Sir Charles had already been a friend for twenty years: we met in San Francisco in the early 70s, and we had collaborated on projects in a number of places, including Carnegie Hall, Chicago, San Francisco and Houston. It was very enjoyable to work with him, especially on such projects as *Iphigénie en Tauride*, *Idomeneo*, *Tristan und Isolde*, and a series of Gilbert and Sullivan recordings, which began in my very first weeks with the Telarc recording of *The Mikado*, and continued with *The Pirates of Penzance*, *HMS Pinafore*, *The Yeomen of the Guard* and *Trial by Jury*.'

Matthew Epstein also found his working relationship with Carlo Rizzi productive and enjoyable, and it began with a memorable meeting. 'Just before I was asked to start at Welsh National Opera I had heard a performance of *Rigoletto* conducted by the young conductor Carlo Rizzi. I went backstage to meet him after the performance, complimented him and told him it was one of the best *Rigolettos* I had ever heard. His remark to me was: '*One* of the best performances of *Rigoletto*?' We laughed about this for years.

'I always find it interesting to sit through auditions with my musical colleagues. With Carlo we never had to say a word to each other. We would turn to each other and look, if we heard a voice we liked. Carlo and I shared a great deal of respect for the old-fashioned Italian tradition of singing and conducting. For me, Carlo is one of the young Italians who represents the rebirth of the old tradition. He is an opera conductor from top to bottom, and has huge respect and knowledge for the old style, rather than the more modern symphonic approach that has taken a strong position in Italy over the past few years. He is also of course an extraordinary conductor of a broad range of repertoire – Britten, Janáček, Strauss and Wagner. I remember with such joy the *Rosenkavalier* we did together. Both of these musical directors were real, strong and responsive colleagues; they were, and have remained, great friends.'

It was during Matthew Epstein's period of tenure that one of the most remarkable guest conductors to work with WNO came to Cardiff.

In my first season, I had the honour of collaborating with Pierre Boulez in Peter Stein's *Pelléas et Mélisande* production. I have never seen such a perfect working relationship between conductor, director and cast. The loving care with which Boulez attended all staging rehearsals, and the loving care with which Peter Stein attended all of Boulez's orchestral rehearsals, was something I've never seen equalled. For me it was a benchmark of how great international opera productions should be put together. Other guest conductors we worked with were Ivor Bolton who made an exciting appearance at WNO doing a production by Tim Albery of *La finta giardiniera*. This was before his career at Munich and Salzburg and on the continent. Another conductor who came into a big career was Mark Minkowski. When we did *Ariodante* I decided to ask him to conduct it. Again, I found him a wonderful collaborator. A third conductor I worked with who was an old friend, was John Nelson who came to conduct the Elijah Moshinsky production of *Beatrice and Benedict,* which opened just after my period at WNO.'

Matthew Epstein appreciated the way in which the WNO staff conductors worked with the musical directors and guest conductors. He also wanted to ensure that the relationship with

former musical directors continued, with Richard Armstrong becoming Principal Guest Conductor for a time, and Sir Charles Mackerras as Conductor Emeritus.

'Having Carlo as Musical Director and Charles and Richard as regular performers with us would be important in maintaining the musical excellence of the Company. That tripartite group gave the possibility of having some excellent guest conductors in the mix, but also kept a strong central core of working relationships.'

Anthony Freud succeeded Matthew Epstein as General Director in 1994. From 1984 to 1992 he had been WNO's Company Secretary and Director of Opera Planning, and from 1992 until his appointment in 1994 he worked in the Netherlands as Executive Producer for Philips Classics. Carlo Rizzi and he had already worked together on Rizzi's first WNO engagement to conduct *The Barber of Seville* in 1991, and later *Count Ory* and *Rigoletto*. Carlo Rizzi's career had concentrated up to that point on the Italian repertory. But once established at WNO, he began to branch out much more widely. Anthony Freud believes this has been beneficial both to Rizzi and to the Company.

'I went backstage to meet him after the performance, complimented him and told him it was one of the best *Rigolettos* I had ever heard.' Matthew Epstein

Carlo Rizzi
Photograph Bill Cooper

The new production of *Eugene Onegin* conducted by Tugan
is a good example of the potential his relationship with the
Company had to offer.' Anthony Freud

Tugan Sokhiev
Photograph Clive Barda

'Both from WNO's and Carlo's points of view, it has been very important both to provide Carlo with repertoire which constitutes his core activity in guest conducting around the world, while at the same time giving him opportunities to conduct operas that he has not yet conducted elsewhere. It offers a mixture of repertoire, combining the core Italian operas with some more unexpected routes – *Elektra*, *Der Rosenkavalier*, *Salome* and *Ariadne auf Naxos*, *Peter Grimes* and *The Turn of the Screw*, *Fidelio* and *Katya Kabanova*. Spring 2006 sees him conducting Bryn Terfel in *The Flying Dutchman,* having conducted *Tristan und Isolde* a few seasons ago. This joint exploration of repertoire has benefited both Carlo, WNO and our audiences: Carlo's performances in such wide-ranging repertoire were immensely distinguished.'

Anthony Freud believes that the continuing relationships with guest conductors is important for the Company's work, and has spent the past fifteen years building such relationships:

'Just as we establish ongoing relationships with important singers and directors, so it's vital to establish ongoing relationships with conductors. I think of it in terms of a flexible artistic family, centred around the Music Director, but involving a flexible and changing but nonetheless identifiable group of conductors, directors and singers. They are an ongoing presence with WNO; their work evolves with WNO; they grow with WNO; they benefit from WNO, and WNO also benefits as a result.'

The partnership between Vladimir Jurowski and Richard Jones yielded such productions as *Hansel and Gretel*, *The Queen of Spades* and, most recently, *Wozzeck*, all three of which won great critical acclaim.

'I'll never forget what Vladimir said to me after the first night of *The Queen of Spades*. He told me he had conducted *The Queen of Spades* in important productions and houses, and he half-thought he had learned all there was to know about it. But his work at WNO with Richard Jones was a revelation; he felt that he had rediscovered the piece. That's a wonderful tribute to the process from a distinguished conductor. The combination of Vladimir, Richard and WNO is a very potent one.'

Vladimir Jurowski also collaborated with Silviu Purcarete in a production of *Parsifal*, which was the first time Jurowski had conducted a Wagner opera. Other guest conductors have also made a huge contribution to WNO's recent work, says Anthony Freud:

'With Robert Spano, the work he did on *Carmen* and *Così fan tutte* made us hear those works anew. Daniel Harding made his British operatic debut in *Jenůfa*. Mark Wigglesworth conducted *Elektra* and *The Rake's Progress* in the 90s, and will return to conduct his first *Tristan* in 2006. Rinaldo Alessandrini's performances in new productions of *The Coronation of Poppea* and *The Marriage of Figaro* were revelatory and we are all looking forward to his return to the Company for *Ulysses* in Autumn 2006. Paul McCreesh's collaboration with Katie Mitchell on *Jephtha* delivered one of the most important landmarks in the Company's repertoire. And Patrick Summers, who conducted the new production of *Rigoletto*, is of course the Music Director of Houston Grand Opera.'

Another guest conductor was a young Russian, Tugan Sokhiev, who came to WNO to conduct *La bohème*. At the end of Carlo Rizzi's tenure as Musical Director with WNO, Tugan Sokhiev was appointed to succeed him, a position he held for two years. Anthony Freud speaks warmly of the appointment:

'When someone said to me "Do you think Tugan has enough experience?" I said "You don't employ a 24 year-old music director for his experience." WNO is a company which has a long and proud tradition of giving exceptional opportunities

Carlo Rizzi
Photograph Neil Bennett

to exceptional artists. It seemed to me that the prospect of an extraordinarily talented young Music Director who may not, by virtue of his youth, have had extensive experience elsewhere, was a very exciting one. Tugan's career and his future plans since he left WNO bear out the level of his talent. The Company and Tugan stood to benefit enormously from the relationship working. It seems with hindsight that WNO is a Company which needed a greater level of experience from its Music Director than Tugan had, and that exceptional talent alone proved not to have been enough.'

Although Tugan Sokhiev conducted a number of operas outside the Russian repertoire, it was his performances of *Eugene Onegin* that were particularly well received:
'The new production of *Eugene Onegin* conducted by Tugan is a good example of the potential his relationship with the Company had to offer. The Chorus and Orchestra were already sounding different, and sounding wonderfully specific in that repertoire. It was a sign of what was possible to achieve over an evolving period, and these things do take time.'

Tugan Sokhiev was succeeded by Carlo Rizzi, who returned to his original position at WNO for the Autumn Season of 2004 to see the Company into its new home. Before the move, Carlo Rizzi conducted a notable new production, by the Australian Neil Armfield, of Strauss's *Ariadne auf Naxos,* as part of the Company's final season at the New Theatre.

Once WNO was in its new home Wales Millennium Centre, Carlo Rizzi inaugurated the Company's first season in residence with performances of *La traviata, Cavalleria rusticana* and *Pagliacci,* which played alongside yet another acclaimed new WNO production from Richard Jones and Vladimir Jurowski of Berg's *Wozzeck.*

The 2005/6 season opened with a long-awaited production of Verdi's grand operatic masterpiece,

Don Carlos. Interviewed as he prepared to leave WNO and take up his new position of General Director of Houston Grand Opera, Anthony Freud felt *Don Carlos* showed the greatest strengths of Welsh National Opera:

'Carlo Rizzi and I have worked together very closely as artistic directors, a partnership in which we have tried together to find ways to lead the development of WNO, taking it to areas where it has not been before. The results of that are palpable. The development of the Orchestra and Chorus has been enormous during Carlo's time as Music Director. The quality of the performances of *Don Carlos* are the most eloquent possible tribute to that evolution and that development. There are some core works in the Company's repertoire which require a maturity of ensemble that can only be achieved by a real company working together on an evolving, continuing basis. *Don Carlos* is a good example of that: it is a piece that requires maturity as well as virtuosity of performance. Our ensemble of Music Director, Chorus and Orchestra collaborated with a depth and an integrity that can only come from longevity of association. It was the most perfect display of this mutually inspiring and productive relationship.'

Home at last

Photographer **Neil Bennett** was given 'Access All Areas' when he joined WNO as it worked towards the opening weekend in its new home in Wales Millennium Centre. Even as the packing cases were being emptied, 250 WNO singers, musicians, technicians and administrators were preparing for one of WNO's most important seasons in 60 years, and Neil was there to capture them on film.

Janáček *The Cunning Little Vixen* 1987

The Sunday Times reviewing the
performances at London's Dominion
Theatre said 'By the end of the opera,
the audience had come to understand and
share the simple but ecstatic acceptance
of change and decay, decay and change,
nobly conveyed by the WNO orchestra
under Richard Armstrong. We are fortunate
that the WNO have found so versatile and
accomplished a Musical Director as
Mr Armstrong'.
Helen Field as Vixen
Photograph Brian Tarr

Productions

The last 20 years have seen some of WNO's most spectacular productions caught in breathtaking still-life by exceptional theatre photographers. From *The Ring* in 1986 to *The Flying Dutchman* in 2006, WNO's outstanding productions have continued to delight, shock, intrigue and beguile its audiences. As you turn the pages and remember, 25 members of WNO, past and present, share their own favourite productions and memories, illustrated with specially-commissioned portraits by **Brian Tarr.**

Humperdinck *Hansel and Gretel* 1998

Awards

WNO has been nominated for, or has won virtually every UK opera prize, including winning the Olivier Award in 1998 and in 1999. In 1999, 2000 and 2001, WNO won the prestigious Royal Philharmonic Society Music Award for Outstanding Achievement in Opera - the only arts organisation ever to have won the Award for three consecutive years.

The first of the acclaimed collaborations for WNO between Richard Jones and Vladimir Jurowski, *Hansel and Gretel* won the Olivier Award for Opera in 1999. In *The Guardian*, Andrew Clements wrote: 'The worlds that Richard Jones creates on the operatic stage linger in the mind long after details of the musical performance have faded.
His remarkable new *Hansel and Gretel* for WNO promised to imprint itself indelibly.'
Imelda Drumm as Hansel and Linda Kitchen as Gretel
Photograph Clive Barda

Berg *Wozzeck* 2005

The partnership of conductor
Vladimir Jurowski and director
Richard Jones, in particular for
Wozzeck, received the Theatrical
Management Association Award for
Achievement in Opera in 2005.
In *The Independent on Sunday*
Anna Picard wrote: 'This is a world-
class ensemble of singing actors in a
world-class production.'
Christopher Purves as Wozzeck and
Gun-Brit Barkmin as Marie
Photograph Bill Cooper

WNO MAX *Katerina* 2004

WNO MAX won the 2004 RPS Award for Education for an innovative large-scale project for 200 primary school children in Merthyr Tydfil, in which they worked with professional artists from WNO to create and perform a new choral opera using Janáček's opera *Katya Kabanova* as inspiration. Composer Ruth Byrchmore and librettist Alan Osborne integrated the children's words and music into their composition. *Katerina* was performed to over 2000 people and was recorded on CD. Two years later, a further 240 children from Denbighshire and Gwynedd worked with WNO to develop and perform their own interpretation of *Katerina*, 1800 people in the audience.
Photograph Brian Tarr

Geraint Talfan Davies
Chairman
With WNO from 2000 to 2003

Favourite production

I have to say that *Jephtha* affected me perhaps more than any opera production I have seen. There can't have been more penetrating performances than those of Mark Padmore and Sarah Tynan as Jephtha and his daughter Iphis. The tension and the dilemmas of the opera tugged at your guts from beginning to end, with an added twist from Katie Mitchell's direction and Vicki Mortimer's set that made those dilemmas contemporary with such masterful under-statement. It was one of those performances when, as the curtain falls, it is difficult to speak and you feel you want to delay the curtain calls for a few minutes to gather yourself.

Best memory

During the WNO MAX *Katerina* project, 200 school children from Merthyr Tydfil came down to WNO in Cardiff – they had been working on their piece which they based on the WNO production of Janáček's *Katya Kabanova*. During the afternoon Anthony Freud and I sat amongst those children during a dress rehearsal of the full opera at the New Theatre. If you had told me beforehand that 200 primary school children would sit through two hours of a Janáček opera I would not have believed you. But there they were, rapt with attention, and when Suzanne Murphy, playing the mother-in-law from hell, came out to take a curtain they booed her loudly in the best panto tradition. It was a moment of such fun and optimism.

The Queen of Spades won the Royal
Philharmonic Society Award and the
Barclays Theatre Award in 2001, both
for Outstanding Achievement
in Opera.
Photograph Clive Barda

Debussy
Pelléas and Mélisande 1992

Pelléas and Mélisande won the
International Classical Music Awards
in 1992. The remarkable pairing of
conductor Pierre Boulez, coming out
of conducting retirement after 12
years, and revered director
Peter Stein was acclaimed in the UK.
However, the crowning triumph came
when WNO took the production to
Le Châtelet in Paris and received
standing ovations. General Director
Matthew Epstein said: 'It shows what
a massive international reputation
we have. Can you imagine La Scala
bringing, say, *Peter Grimes* to London,
or the Dresden Company bringing
Tippett to Cardiff? We took Debussy
to Paris and had them calling
for more.'
Neill Archer as Pelléas and
Alison Hagley as Mélisande
Photograph Clive Barda

Poulenc *The Carmelites* 1999

Phyllida Lloyd's production won the Royal Philharmonic Society Music Award for Outstanding Achievement in Opera during 1999 – won jointly with ENO as co-producers. Commenting on the intimacy of the New Theatre compared with the Coliseum, Rodney Milnes wrote in *The Times*: 'the impact of the work was immeasurably greater simply because of the comparative intimacy of Cardiff's New Theatre. The nuns' resuming their Salve Regina fortissimo after the first thump of the guillotine was simply heart-rending.'
Elizabeth Vaughan as The Prioress and Sally Burgess as Mother Marie
Photograph Clive Barda

Monteverdi
The Coronation of Poppea 1997

David Alden's production of *The Coronation of Poppea* has
brought WNO more awards than any other production –
it won the Evening Standard Award, and was cited in the
WNO's awards from the Royal Philharmonic Society and
Barclays Theatre Awards.
Neil Jenkins as Arnalta (below)
Photograph Clive Barda

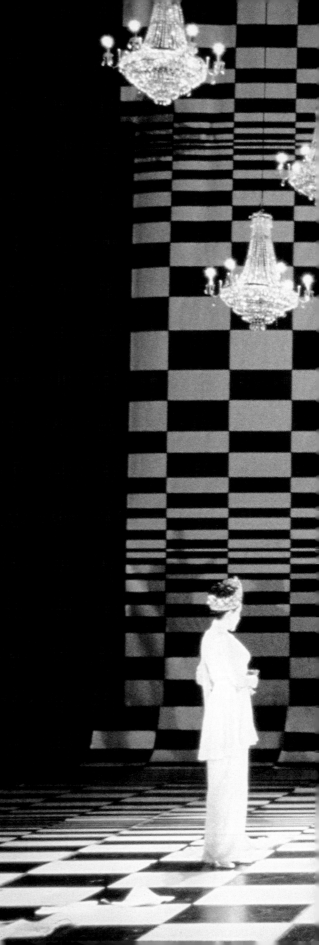

Mozart *La clemenza di Tito* 1997

WNO won the Laurence Olivier Award
for its performances of *La clemenza
di Tito* at the Shaftesbury Theatre in
London. The last opera to be written
by Mozart, it was written in Prague
during the period when *The Magic
Flute* was in its first rehearsals
in Vienna, some of it during the
composer's coach journey between
the two cities.
Katarina Karnéus as Sesto and
Isabelle Vernet as Vitellia
Photograph Clive Barda

Bizet *Carmen* 1997

Patrice Caurier and Moshe Leiser's production of *Carmen* won the Barclays Theatre Award for Outstanding Achievement in Opera in 1997. Rodney Milnes wrote in *The Times* 'This WNO *Carmen* is strikingly fresh. Every note, every word has been weighted and considered anew. There is no hint of tradition or routine. You may not agree with everything that happens, but you have to admire the painstaking preparation, the questioning intelligence behind it all. One to remind you that as well as being one of the most popular of all operas, *Carmen* in its indefinable multifacetedness is also one of the greatest.'
The Chorus of Welsh National Opera and boys from The Bishop of Llandaff Church in Wales High School
2004 revival
Photograph Brian Tarr

The Orchestra of WNO won the Royal
Philharmonic Society Music Award in the
Large Ensemble category as it celebrated
its Silver Jubilee, 25 years after it had
been formed in 1970.
Conductor Carlo Rizzi
Photograph Brian Tarr

The Orchestra of Welsh National Opera 1995

The Orchestra of Welsh National Opera
in rehearsal in its new home,
Wales Millennium Centre.
Photograph Neil Bennett

Handel *Ariodante* 1994

Composers

Over the years, WNO has performed many works by a number of significant composers – Beethoven, Britten, Handel, Janáček, Mozart, Puccini, Verdi and Wagner. By grouping productions by composer, the extraordinary variety of production and design styles becomes apparent, as WNO tries to ensure that no approach to a production is the same as any other, whether they are period or contemporary.

Andrew Clements wrote in *The Guardian*: 'Ariodante is one of the greatest of baroque operas and in David Alden's staging, it receives a theatrical and musical treatment fully worthy of its stature.' David Alden's *Ariodante* opened ten days after his identical twin brother Christopher Alden opened his new production of *Turandot* for WNO. Della Jones as Ariodante
Photograph Catherine Ashmore

Beethoven *Fidelio* 1997

Suzanne Murphy as Leonore,
Rebecca Evans as Marzelline and
Donald Macintyre as Rocco
Photograph Bill Cooper

Beethoven only wrote one opera, but revised it so thoroughly that the two main versions are often given different names; *Leonore* which premièred in Vienna in 1805, and the later version *Fidelio* which opened in 1814. Patrice Caurier and Moshe Leiser created a new production of *Fidelio* for WNO in 1997.

Later that year, the WNO Chorus went as the guest chorus to Le théâtre de *Champs-Elysées* in Paris, performing *Fidelio* and *Leonore* on consecutive nights through a week-long season. In 2001, Caurier and Leiser returned to WNO to direct a new production of Leonore.

Beethoven *Leonore* 2001

The men of the Chorus of WNO
Photograph Clive Barda

John Hayel
Master Carpenter
Started with WNO's sister Drama Company in 1974; with WNO since 1982

Favourite opera

Billy Budd probably – I wasn't brought up on opera but when we first did *Billy Budd*, in Michael Geliot's production, it was built like a real sailing ship so it was built with full naval rigging. It is a real man's opera – no women in the cast - and it tells a great story. That first production had some great singers in it too, like Tom Allen.

Favourite production

The other *Billy Budd* we did, directed by Neil Armfield. The set is a great piece of engineering and I felt I was really involved in its creation from the start. The designer Brian Thomson came up with a brilliant moving platform for the decks of the ship. All the crew were on stage as sailors, and we chose two of our guys who were great at computer games to control the moving platforms. It needed their soft touch on the joysticks of the hydraulic control. It was a high-pressure show, but we all really enjoyed it.

Best memory

The trip to Milan in 1989. I don't think people realised how big that tour would be for us. We played *Falstaff* in a theatre across the road from La Scala, and at the end of the show the Italian audience just erupted – Peter Stein had said to us that we would be walking into the lion's den, but they just loved it. To go to Milan and be a success there was really something - everyone had a grin on their face. Thinking back now about that moment on stage, it was just amazing.

On Neil Armfield's production, Michael White wrote in *The Independent on Sunday*: 'For me, *Budd* is one of the great works of lyric theatre. Its torrential confluence of beauty, power and anguish leaves me on my knees. And after the first night of Welsh National Opera's lacerating new production, I wasn't the only member of the audience to feel like crawling out into the streets of Cardiff. It was that good.'
Photograph Bill Cooper

Britten *Billy Budd* 1998

Ian Douglas
Company Manager
With WNO since 1977

Favourite opera

If pushed, I would say *Peter Grimes*.
The music is searingly beautiful at
times, and Britten's music evokes the
setting and story perfectly. But *Billy
Budd* pushes it very close. It was one
of the first operas I ever worked on
in Michael Geliot's production with
a great cast including Thomas Allen,
Nigel Douglas and Forbes Robinson.
If *Billy Budd* and *Peter Grimes* could
ever be recognised as a double bill
– which is a bit difficult – then First
Place would be assured!

Best memory

I have lots, but to see a full house
coming into the theatre is a great
thrill, and if they have a great
evening to overhear them raving
about it in a local pub or restaurant
after the show is fantastic. Of course
the reverse can be among the worst
moments: being at any performance
with a poor house is so dispiriting
for everybody, in the Company, in the
audience and theatre staff.

Britten *Peter Grimes* 1999

Peter Grimes was the last of
Peter Stein's productions for WNO.
Michael Kennedy wrote in *The Sunday
Telegraph:* 'If one thought one had
become inured through familiarity
to the dramatic and emotional
impact of this work, this was a
performance to take one back to raw
first impressions. The storm nearly
blew us out of our seats, the Borough
inhabitants' manhunt cries of
'Peter Grimes' froze the blood – what
a chorus – and their persecution of
Ellen Orford in Act 2 was almost
as vicious.'
Photograph Bill Cooper

Britten *The Turn of the Screw* 2000

Roderic Dunnett wrote in *The Independent*: 'Only last season, WNO showed the clear advantages of letting operas speak for themselves. Now they have done it again, serving up a straight-lined, skilfully lit, focused and incisive production of *The Turn of the Screw*, whose simple unfussy approach and determined lack of tinkering would have had the composer positively purring. Carlo Rizzi is unafraid to let rip with his 13 players, who sometimes sound more like 26. The playing was of the highest order.'
Paul Nilon as Peter Quint,
Oliver Carden as Miles and
Janice Watson as The Governess
Photograph Bill Cooper

Handel *Jephtha* 2003

Katie Mitchell created an operatic
staging of Handel's last oratorio.
Conductor Paul McCreesh said:
'One of the things that drew me to
this project was the thought of the
WNO Chorus giving some serious
stick to these fantastic choruses.
The WNO Chorus is one of the great
things of British music-making. It
is fantastic to enjoy this brilliant,
rich, passionate, committed, vibrant,
exciting sound, and to hear this
sound grafted onto Handel's music.'
Mark Padmore as Jephtha and
Sarah Tynan as Iphis
Photograph Clive Barda

Tony Lewis
Chairman
With WNO since 2003

Favourite opera

I think probably *Eugene Onegin* grabs all my senses. And makes me realise that opera is really a massive team game – with an opera like this you push the theatre, acting and movement side of things, and extend that as much as you do the singing and the playing. It is a highly emotional opera too. Wonderful!

Favourite production

Jephtha was absolutely fantastic, with all those beautiful musical ornaments and so gloriously sung. It had elements of Greek chorus in it, a mystical feeling leading towards the ladder to heaven in the end. It was all so beautifully pulled together, it really worked wonderfully.

Best memory

One tends to toy with the same operas over the years, but when you come suddenly on a new one it is quite amazing. That happened to me with *Wozzeck* on our opening weekend in Wales Millennium Centre. It was a shattering experience, a bit bleak, but outstanding. That is absolutely where we should be as a company, pushing the boundaries.

Musical Opinion said: 'Janáček's adaptation of Dostoyevsky's short novel is harsh and unrelenting and David Pountney's grim production rightly emphasises these qualities. The final scene, with all the prisoners marching uniformly round the set demonstrates the complete hopelessness of their situation as depicted by both musician and author and its effect is quite devastating. It was such a strong performance, that in spite of the grimness of the piece, its essential humanity shone through.'
Photograph Roger de Woolf

Christopher Hodges
Sub Principal Cellist
With WNO since 1979

Favourite opera

It would probably be *From the House of the Dead* by Janáček - although it isn't a long opera, it is an intensely dramatic experience because it runs without a break. It is set in a very harsh setting, almost a concentration camp. It's about the stories of the criminals who are incarcerated there. The stories link up in a clever way and you don't realise how they are going to link up until the end. And the music, although it is a dour tragic story, I think it is Janáček's best - soaring, lyrical, it's just passionate in that way he has. Plus it's a story of hope and redemption because the bird they capture, an eagle, flies away at the end - it gives them all hope of freedom. For me it is an overwhelming experience - for the orchestra it's hard work but you get wrapped up in this wonderful operatic experience and you come out of it quite drained. That one symbolised opera at its best.

Favourite memory

My best memories are the musical memories. As an orchestral player we are privileged to play terrific music and, though it depends on what mood you are in, I think you always enjoy playing. You always get something from it or there is no point in being there really.

Mozart based his opera on the Beaumarchais play of the same name. Neil Armfield has directed both the opera and the play. He said: 'What I have found every time I have revived either the play or the opera is that both works contain an incredible love of life, and the possibilities of the human imagination. There is an authentic sense of the way that people in power behave and how the concentric ripples around that source of energy have to keep their dance alive in order to survive. In the end the wonderful thing about revivals is the sense that each performance is on the shoulders of the one before, so that the work can only get richer.' Imelda Drumm as Cherubino, Geraldine McGreevy as The Countess, and Nuccia Focile as Susanna

Photograph Bill Cooper

Mozart *The Marriage of Figaro* 2001

As with many of his operas, Calixto Bieito's new production in 2000 caused a rush of condemnation of his explicitly-simulated sex scenes. WNO declared it to be unsuitable for children, but Anthony Freud defended this position. He said: 'In our view the production is true to the spirit of the piece. The opera is about sexual relations – the libretto is full of innuendo which the production reflects.' Neal Davies as Guglielmo, Donald Maxwell as Don Alfonso and Gregory Turay as Ferrando Photograph Bill Cooper

Mozart *Cosi fan tutte* 2000

Russell Moreton
Music Staff
With WNO since 1985

Favourite opera

Definitely *Cosi fan tutte* for me.
There is just sheer quality in the
music which is simply sublime. More
deeply, what attracts me is the way
that Mozart manages to transform
what is ostensibly a trivial plot
and situation into something that
manages to explore every aspect of
human relationships with painful
accuracy. But he still manages to
make us laugh at the characters and
ourselves. *Figaro* is perhaps more
perfect in a way, but *Cosi* just does
it for me.

Favourite production

Of all our productions, the one I had
the best time working on was Robert
Carson's production of *Cendrillon.*

I had never worked on any Massenet
before and we just had a ball.
Patrick Fournillier was conducting
and we had a fabulous cast
– Rebecca Evans, Felicity Palmer,
Lilian Watson, Donald Maxwell. It
was a very good, stylish, touching
production, but the box dance was
particularly entertaining. The ladies
of the chorus had to dance with
boxes containing dresses – but
sometimes they didn't have the right
box, so they had to dress on stage
into a dress which wasn't their own.
Sometimes there were some larger
ladies with tears of laughter rolling
down their cheeks as they couldn't
get into these dresses. We had a
fabulous time all the way through.

The plot of *Idomeneo* is very like the *Jephtha* story – centred round the return of the King of Crete from the Trojan Wars, and around his vow to sacrifice the first living creature he meets on arriving safely home.

The 1991 production was conducted by Sir Charles Mackerras and directed by Howard Davies.

Designer William Dudley created a set which featured flowing water in its original version and soaking wet costumes for the shipwrecked chorus.

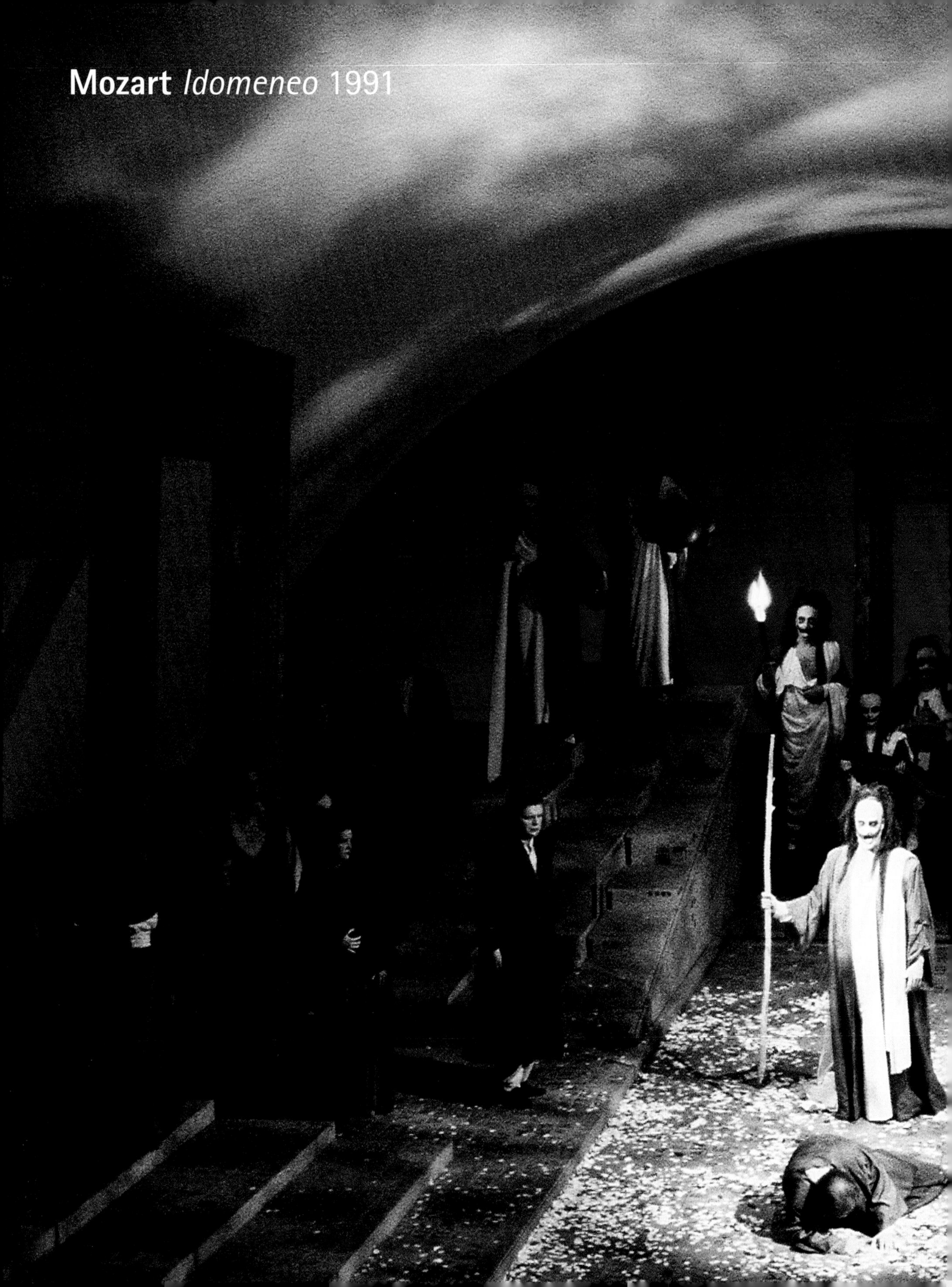
Mozart *Idomeneo* 1991

Don Giovanni was the first opera
to be directed by Katie Mitchell, a
celebrated young theatre director.
According to *The Sunday Times*
'Mitchell inspires her cast to achieve
the kind of subtle, undemonstrative,
unoperatic acting one expects as
a matter of course in the spoken
theatre but rarely encounters in the
opera house. Body language and eye
contact are paramount in this subtle,
intimate staging.'
Catrin Wyn-Davies as Zerlina and
Davide Damiani as Don Giovanni
Photograph Bill Cooper

Of the 1990 revival of Giles Havergal's 1987 production, Kenneth Loveland, writing in *Opera* magazine, observed: 'If ever there was a performance which stated a clear case for presenting opera in a language the local audience could understand, this was it. The result was gales of laughter where there might have been merely chuckles while the next aria was awaited, and at the very end, an uproarious ovation from a packed audience which had obviously enjoyed every minute.'
Bryn Terfel as Figaro,
Anne Dawson as Susanna,
Dorothy Hood as Marcellina and
Geoffrey Moses as Bartolo
1990 revival
Photograph Brian Tarr

Mozart *The Marriage of Figaro* 1987

Michael Spray
Head of Lighting and Sound
With WNO since 1973

Favourite opera

Definitely *La bohème* - no matter
what type of production you see or
who is the director, the music from
beginning to end is enjoyable and
unforgettable. It's an opera about life.

Favourite production

Lucian Pintilie's *Carmen* in 1983
- this controversial production was
the best piece of theatre I have
ever seen. Lucian's visual concept
of Bizet's music is awesome. From
the first note of the overture to the
final blackout there is action. Radu
Boruzescu's set was simple yet full
of surprises with its revolving floor
and central hydraulic cage, and
John Waterhouse's lighting, from
under floor strip lights to electronic
camera flashes, all became part of
the music. The purists hated it and
the uninitiated loved it. This was the
stuff of legend. In 1986 we took it
to Vancouver for Expo 86. The press
conference after the performance was
packed to the doors. The surprising
thing was that it was the older
element of the audience who loved
the new revitalised idea. And the
young and upwardly mobile who
where outraged and purist.
A complete reverse from our British
tour. For me it was a monumental
leap forward for WNO.

In 2001, Roderic Dunnett wrote in
The Independent: 'Katie Mitchell's
production is as pure as the free air
where Katya craves to soar; seagull-
like, in her rapt Bartokian vision
(Janáček's accompanying sequence of
bassoon, horn, flutes, flickering harp,
solo violin and cellos mesmerised.)
Vicki Mortimer's opening set, neatly
revisited at the close, is a café that
looks a cross between a waiting
room and sanatorium. Behind the
Volga meanders, a serpent awaiting
its prey. An inspired evening.'
Suzanne Murphy as Kabanicha,
Alan Fairs as Dikoy and
Nuccia Focile as Katya
Photograph Ivan Kyncl

Janáček *Katya Kabanova* 2001

Domini Lipman
Viola Player
With WNO since 1979

Favourite opera

I rather have favourite periods in opera. I like Janáček and Britten, and the earlier period of Handel. Also late Verdi operas. Part of my fondness for Janáček and Britten is that they both work so well for the viola. Britten was himself a viola player. He wrote a spectacular viola solo in *Peter Grimes*, and Janáček wrote an obbligato part for an early instrument called a viola d'amore in his opera *Katya Kabanova*. They both chose very powerful stories of the human condition for their libretti.

Best memory

Certainly one of the funniest memories came in the production of *Pelléas and Mélisande*, conducted by Pierre Boulez. It included in the cast two doves. They duly arrived with a very pleasant trainer who told us how experienced they were and always responded to his call. The first night arrived and the doves appeared on stage: one immediately flew into the circle and landed on the balcony. After a few minutes we could hear the Company Manager, Barbara Stuart, on her crackling walkie-talkie saying 'whereabouts of dove unknown'. Eventually they located the dove which took one look at the trainer and thought 'crikey, I should be on stage!' It flew back, briefly settling on Boulez's shoulder before returning to the stage as the curtain came down!

The 2003 revival of Katie Mitchell's
1998 *Jenůfa* saw the last opera
performances by soprano
Susan Chilcott before her untimely
death later that year. In *The
Sunday Telegraph*, Michael Kennedy
wrote: 'I doubt if I have heard a
greater performance of the music
of *Jenůfa* than that given under
Sir Charles Mackerras's direction at
the New Theatre. Susan Chilcott, in a
compelling, touching and beautifully
sung portrayal of the title role,
responded with every fibre of her
being to the conductor's inspiration.'
Nigel Robson as Laca, Susan Chilcott
as Jenůfa and Peter Wedd as Števa
2003 revival
Photograph Clive Barda

Janáček *Jenůfa* 1998

Janáček
From the House of the Dead 1982

Lord Davies
Board member since 1973 until present
Chairman from 1975 to 2000

Favourite opera

I love *The Marriage of Figaro*, and *Der Rosenkavalier* – if they are done right they are fantastic – and I love *La bohème*. They have all got such gorgeous music.

Favourite production

The most thrilling first night was Serban's production of *Eugene Onegin* with Josephine Barstow and Thomas Allen. Particularly the Letter Scene – the scenery was sparce, just with a window hanging, but it was absolutely electric. Lensky's aria too was superb, sung by Anthony Rolfe Johnson.

Best memory

I suppose one of the great occasions was WNO's performance of *Götterdämmerung* at the Royal Opera House, after which I was able to give a party for the Company in the Crush Bar – it was a very special night for everyone.

Worst memory

There was an occasion in the mid-80s when we were told we wouldn't be getting any increase in funding from the Arts Councils, and we had to say we were going to close the company – that was very tough. But it did persuade them to sort something out.

Mozart *The Magic Flute* 2005

Director Dominic Cooke worked closely with designer Julian Crouch and costume designer Kevin Pollard to create a magical world, inspired by the work of the artist Magritte. He said: 'I've always loved Magritte's work: it's populist and accessible at the same time as being disturbing and challenging.

We found ourselves looking at Magritte's paintings for textures rather than a complete world: his is a crazy world of dream, of subconscious and juxtaposition. We felt that in a world inspired by Magritte we would be able to be more fluid and playful.'
Photograph Bill Cooper

Madam Butterfly is the oldest
production still in the WNO
repertoire. Premièred in 1978,
Director Joachim Herz and WNO's
Head of Music Julian Smith worked
together to create a revised version
of the opera, going back to Puccini's
original scores and libretto. In 2004,
the revival conducted by Julian Smith
celebrated the centenary of the
opera's première in 1904.

Nuccia Focile as Cio–Cio–San and
Mathew Welch as Trouble
2004 revival
Photograph Brian Tarr

Puccini *Madam Butterfly* 1978

Paul Gyton
Tenor, WNO Chorus
With WNO since 1977

Favourite opera

La bohème has a very special place in my heart not only because it has such beautiful music, laughter and sadness, but because it was during our current production that I met my wife, Alwyn Mellor, who was singing Musetta at the time. It moves me to tears every time I see or hear it and had it not been for *La bohème*, I might not have met Alwyn.

Favourite production

It has to be a dead heat for me. For excitement and pride in our achievement it would be the Michael Geliot production of *Billy Budd*. The set was just like HMS Victory cut in half – it had real hammocks, naval rigging and canons you could sit on. And a fabulous cast including Thomas Allen, Forbes Robinson and Nigel Douglas.

But I also loved Matthew Warchus's production of *The Rake's Progress*. I particularly liked the way that time went backwards – the clock would go into reverse and so did the people on stage. It had everything from the exciting roaring boys and brothel scene to the sad and deeply moving bedlam scene. It gave the public a real treat!

Puccini *La bohème* 1984

Through all its revivals since it was first produced in 1984, Göran Järvefelt's production has maintained his central ideal. He said: 'For a production of *La bohème* to be believable, it has to be cast with young singers. I have been lucky enough to get this requirement fulfilled every time I have directed the piece.'
Alwyn Mellor as Mimì and Gwyn Hughes Jones as Rodolfo
1999 revival
Photograph Brian Tarr

Puccini *La fanciulla del West* 1991

In *Opera* magazine Hugh Canning
wrote: 'Julian Smith was always,
even in Richard Armstrong's day,
the company's expert Puccinian and
he conducted this most fascinating,
orchestrally most impressionistic of
Puccini's scores, with a keen ear for
the almost Debussian textures of
the music.'
Suzanne Murphy as Minnie and
Dennis O'Neill as Dick Johnson
Photograph Clive Barda

John Abendstern
Timpanist
With WNO since 1985

Favourite opera

You take different things from different operas, but I think I would choose *Parsifal* as my favourite as it contains such strong themes. I listened to it first on a coach trip to Birmingham, and I was almost in a cold sweat because it was just so gripping. I was greatly moved by the personal journeys of the main characters as they strove towards forgiveness and enlightenment, coupled with Wagner's wonderful score. It has amazing themes to it.

Favourite productions

I only get to see the productions in Bristol or Oxford when we (the orchestra) are in front of the stage. *Otello* was an example of WNO firing on all cylinders – the staging, costumes, lighting, cast and Peter Stein's direction combined to produce a superb ensemble piece. It was televised, and if you were to freeze the tape at any point, it just looks like the most beautiful painting.

Also, anything conducted by Sir Charles Mackerras.

Michael Clifton Thompson
Tenor, WNO Chorus
With WNO since 1985

Favourite opera

It has to be *Tosca*. The combined power of the music and drama takes the audience through the whole spectrum of emotions as the story unfolds. It leaves one completely drained at the tragic end.

Favourite production

Cendrillon, produced by Robert Carson in 1993. We performed this at the New Theatre in December. It was an inspired, funny and magical production with many coups-de-théâtre. We all left the theatre feeling totally uplifted by the experience.

Best memory

Foreign tours are always a great time for company bonding, and I particularly loved going to Japan in 1989. This was such a fantastic opportunity to visit a country so different to ours. The city of Tokyo was an experience in itself with its vast population. Most memorable for me were the temples and shrines in Kyoto and our trip to Mount Fuji where we stayed in a Japanese hotel. Here we had our own personal maid who brought us our breakfast of green tea and a selection of boiled and smoked fish at 8am. Then into our en-suite stone bath fed by the hot spring waters of Mount Fuji – hedonistic or what!

In *The Financial Times*, Andrew Clements wrote: 'The essence of Michael Blakemore's approach to his first opera is faithful historical realism. In one sense, it is almost super-real, for Ashley Martin–Davis's sets are dominated by vivid, larger-than-life icons. The battlements of Act 3 are capped by a massive, swooping angel, avenging sword in hand.'
2001 revival
Photograph Bill Cooper

Puccini *Turandot* 1994

On the setting for *Turandot*, Director Christopher Alden said: '*Turandot* was written at the start of the Mussolini era, and I think that in a lot of the piece Puccini was expressing his feelings about what was going on inside and outside Italy, couching them in orientalist terms, but giving what can be read as images of Fascist crowd-control and mass hysteria. We have dressed the chorus for the crowd scenes as 'barbarian bourgeoisie' – a cross between a mythological orient and the kind of clothes middle class people would wear in Mussolini's era, people who actively supported a monstrous regime.'

2004 revival
Photograph Brian Tarr

Otello was the first of four acclaimed and award-winning productions for WNO by director Peter Stein. In *The Guardian* Tom Sutcliffe wrote: 'This production is not just good, it is great. It wears the tradition of operatic Otellos lightly. It is a very beautiful production, both visually and in its dramatic achievement, but it is most mature and accomplished in its ability to exploit expressive elements and concepts without being hag-ridden by them. Once again, WNO have triumphed. This time the triumph will be international.'

Jeffrey Lawton as Otello
Photograph Brian Tarr

Verdi *Otello* 1986

John Stein
Leader of The Orchestra of WNO
With WNO since 1970

Favourite production

Verdi's *Otello*, the first of Peter Stein's WNO productions. The stage set was 'framed' and as the drama progressed from the large chorus opening to the final scene between Otello and Desdemona, the frame size reduced, emphasising the intensity of the relationship between the principal characters. Quite wonderful!

Best memory

Having been instrumental in the formation of a permanent orchestra for WNO, with the then Music Director James Lockhart, I feel a sense of pride in the orchestra's many achievements over the years.

Worst memory

The Hadid opera house debacle and the choice between a rugby stadium and an opera house. If it had been Milan, it would have been like asking the Italians if they wanted La Scala or AC Milan. To choose between the two would be unthinkable. Why not have both? We now have the magnificent WMC of course, but it's not quite the same as having our own 'house'.

Verdi *Falstaff* 1988

Falstaff saw the return to WNO of Peter Stein after the international acclaim for his production of Otello. *Falstaff* not only toured WNO's regular theatres, it also performed at the Royal Opera House, Covent Garden, as well as in Milan, Tokyo and at the Brooklyn Academy of Music in New York. The revival in 1993, with Bryn Terfel taking over the role of Ford, was presented at the Edinburgh International Festival.

Donald Maxwell as Falstaff,
Suzanne Murphy as Alice,
Nuccia Focile as Nannetta,
Wendy Verco as Meg,
Cynthia Buchan as Mrs Quickly
Photograph Catherine Ashmore

Verdi *La traviata* 2004

Directors Patrice Caurier and Moshe
Leiser's contemporary production
of *La traviata* premièred in summer
2004. It was revived in spring 2005,
conducted by Carlo Rizzi, and was
WNO's opening performance in Wales
Millennium Centre on 18 February
when it was televised live on S4C
and relayed live to big screens in
Caernarfon and Aberystwyth.
Photograph Clive Barda

Reviewing Göran Järvefelt's production, in *The Sunday Times* David Cairns wrote: 'Welsh National Opera's *Traviata* is worth travelling a very long way to hear. I cannot recall a *Traviata* equal to it. In the hands of Mackerras and the excellent WNO Orchestra the piece glows with life and unsuspected colour.'
Photograph Clive Barda

Verdi *La traviata* 1988

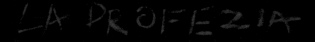

Verdi *Nabucco* 1995

Since 1952, when WNO gave the opera's first UK performance in over a century, *Nabucco* has played an important role in WNO's history. Writing in *The Times* about the 1995 production, Rodney Milnes observed: 'When Carlo Rizzi is on the sort of form that he struck for Tuesday's opening of the WNO season, there are few to beat him in early Verdi. The chorus surpassed themselves: as *Va pensiero*, quite wonderfully sung, faded from a thread of sound into nothingness, the audience was held in breathless silence. There are certain things you just don't applaud, and this was one of them.' Photograph Bill Cooper

Verdi *Simon Boccanegra* 1997

Simon Rees, WNO's Dramaturg, has
the task of explaining operatic plots
to audiences. In the programme
for *Simon Boccanegra* he wrote:
'*Boccanegra* has the reputation for
having a difficult plot, though it is
certainly no more complicated than
some feature films.'
Nuccia Focile as Amelia
Photograph Clive Barda

Andy John
Senior Prop Technician
With WNO since 1980

Favourite opera

The Pearl Fishers as I love Bizet, and any Verdi with our Chorus.

Favourite production

Definitely *From the House of the Dead* and *Peter Grimes*, but probably it has to be *Jephtha* – not necessarily my favourite musically, but it was the total theatre experience, and the emotional quality was just amazing.

Best memory

Peter Grimes – I hadn't been looking forward to this production much. All the other Peter Stein productions – *Otello, Falstaff, Pelléas* etc. – had put the company under enormous pressure, meaning we were eating and sleeping the production for weeks on end. But with *Grimes*, it felt different for me – it was still a lot of hard work but everything just seemed to click in a way that it hadn't for the other shows, and I thought the result was simply fantastic.

Verdi *Rigoletto* 2002

James Macdonald's 2002 production of *Rigoletto* updated the setting from 16th century Mantua to the 1960s White House – the era of John F. Kennedy. In *The Western Mail* Mike Smith wrote: 'Here the updating, if you excuse the pun, hits the mark. Clearly JFK fits fine into the role of the Duke; a character oozing power, charisma and an uncontrolled sexual appetite.' Photograph Bill Cooper

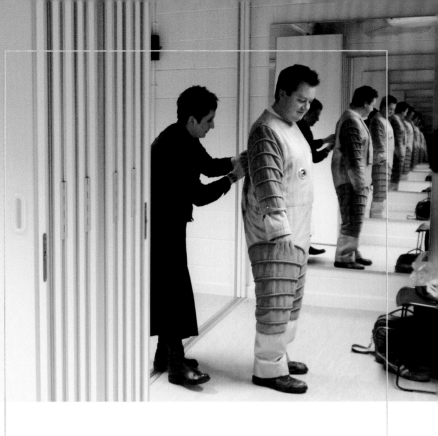

Siân Price
Deputy Head of Costume/Men's Cutter
With WNO since 1979

Best memory
Meeting and working with designer, the late Maria Bjørnson. Each one of her shows was different but at the same time they were all Maria. Her shows for WNO included *The Makropolous Case*, *Katya Kabanova*, *From the The House of the Dead*, *The Cunning Little Vixen* and *Ernani*, though most of them were revivals when I worked on them.

Worst memory
There was a flash flood in July 2001. We watched the water rising in the basement and were able to do nothing to stop it. The following morning, to see the pans of costumes and boxes of shoes floating in the water was such a sad sight.

We then spent four days emptying the basement of 485 pans of costumes of which we could only put six at a time in the lift, as they weighed too much. The Technical Assistants and the ten or so casual crew were fantastic.

Anthony Freud and Carlo Rizzi planned for over ten years to stage the five-act version of *Don Carlos* in French. Always planned for the ever-shifting opening seasons in WNO's new home, *Don Carlos* opened WNO's 60th anniversary season in autumn 2005. Director John Caird's enthusiasm for the opera matched theirs. He said: 'The miracle of this opera for me is that Verdi is so ambitious, in the prime of his power as an artist, that he takes on this massive story, and does it with such grace and authority, and yet every time the music changes it seems to come from his characters, not from him. Every time it seems as if something in the character's mind has conjured up the music from the orchestra. The true greatness of the dramatic artist is in his humility towards his characters.'
Photograph Bill Cooper

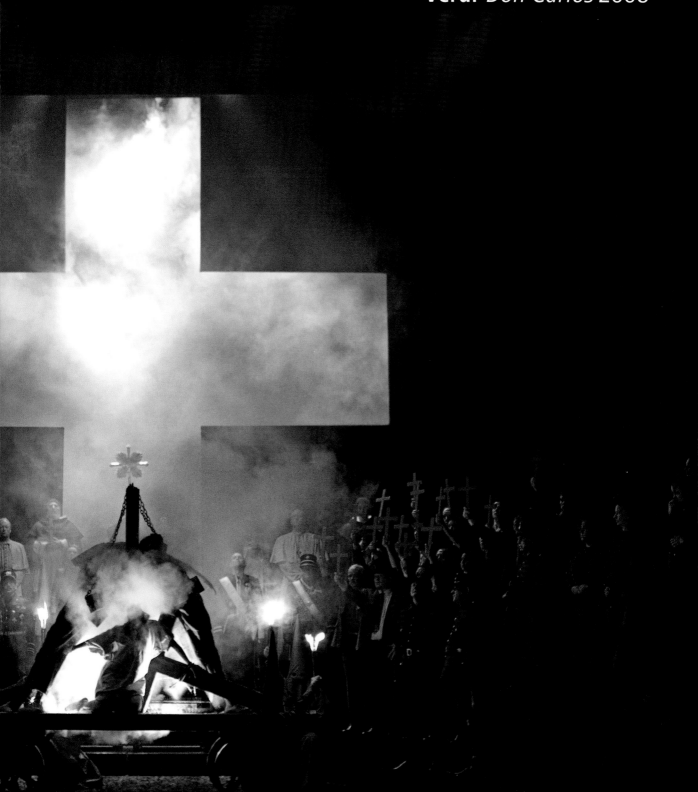

Verdi *Don Carlos* 2005

Scott Hendricks as Posa
Guang Yang as Princesse Eboli
Photograph Bill Cooper

Anthony Freud
Company Secretary and Director of Opera Planning from 1984 to 1992,
General Director from 1994 to 2005

Favourite opera
Don Carlos – an opera which I have
felt passionately about for over
thirty years. From my first day as
General Director, Carlo Rizzi and
I shared that dream of mounting
the piece, so it was from the start
the personification of our working
partnership. We realised that with
the new home on the horizon it
would have been pointless to put
it on before it was a reality – with
the much-postponed opening of the
opera house, it became a much-
postponed production. In the end we
did produce a fantastic production by
John Caird in autumn 2005, ironically
at the start of my last season with

WNO. So it represents not only my
passion for the piece and my belief
in the five-act French version of
the piece we mounted, but also my
partnership with Carlo and my career
with WNO in a way that for me is
very emotional and powerful.

Favourite memory
The opening of the WNO's first season
in Wales Millennium Centre. We all
had to pinch ourselves to believe that
we had finally arrived in our new
home which had a theatre of truly
world-class quality from an acoustic,
visual and technical point of view.

Wagner *The Ring Cycle* 1986
The Rhinegold
Eirian Davies, Deborah Stuart-Roberts and Patricia Bardon as The Rhinedaughters
Photograph Clive Barda

In September 1986, WNO became the first British opera company to tour the full *Ring Cycle*. Opening in Cardiff, it went to the Royal Opera House, Covent Garden (where it sold out on the day booking opened), to the Birmingham Hippodrome and the Bristol Hippodrome. In the *Daily Telegraph* Robert Henderson wrote: 'the entire venture stands forth proudly as a noble vindication of the challenge daringly accepted by the WNO, not only in undertaking the mammoth task of staging Wagner's wepic tetralogy, but also in bringing to the Royal Opera House the first *Ring* in English that has been heard there since the opening decade of the century.'

Wagner *The Ring Cycle* 1986
The Valkyrie

Philip Joll as Wotan and
Anne Evans as Brünnhilde
Photograph Catherine Ashmore

Wagner *The Ring Cycle* 1986
Siegfried

Left: Jeffrey Lawton as Siegfried
Below: Nicholas Folwell as Alberich
Photograph Clive Barda

Wagner *The Ring Cycle* 1986
Götterdämmerung

Anne Evans as Brünnhilde
Photograph Catherine Ashmore

Julia Carson Sims
Stage Manager
With WNO since 1984

Favourite opera

Though I think my perfect opera is probably *Elektra*, *Götterdämmerung* is top of my favourites list. I grew up in a house where Wagner was constantly playing, so I was delighted to be asked to run the Wagner operas for WNO. I did *Siegfried* and *Götterdämmerung* which gave me the chance to work with the late Göran Järvefelt. *Götterdämmerung* gave me one of the 'magic moments' of my career, which was to hear Anne Evans sing the entire role of Brünnhilde in this opera for the first time at the dress rehearsal. Bizarrely, she mostly sat in a chair, as her ankle had been injured in rehearsal – Jeffrey Lawton as Siegfried had wrestled her to the ground a little too realistically and he couldn't hear her shouting above the music. To have been there at her first Brünnhilde was special indeed.

Favourite moment

Perhaps it was the curtain call when we did *The Ring Cycle* at Covent Garden. As at Bayreuth but unusual in Britain, Richard Armstrong, our then Music Director, invited all technical staff to join the call. I took my bow on the stage of Covent Garden knowing my Wagner-loving Dad was out there cheering with the rest. *The Ring* was our first visit to Covent Garden, and it was a massive success – as one of my colleagues said: 'the little Welsh rugby team came and played with the big boys, and we showed them how it is done!' I think their technical staff were impressed by the degree of co-operation between departments, which comes from years of touring together.

WNO took *Tristan und Isolde* to the Royal Opera House, Covent Garden. In *The Sunday Telegraph* Michael Kennedy wrote: 'Last Monday was one of Covent Garden's great evenings and ironically, it was provided by Welsh National Opera's production of *Tristan und Isolde* first heard in Cardiff. Suffice it to say that it sounded and looked even better in the Royal Opera House, thanks not least to Sir Charles Mackerras's masterful conducting which encompassed every degree of light and shade. Crowning all was Anne Evans's Isolde, a personal triumph on a grand scale.'

Jeffrey Lawton as Tristan and Anne Evans as Isolde
Photograph Clive Barda

Wagner *Tristan und Isolde* 1993

Anthony Negus
Senior member of Music Staff and Conductor
With WNO since 1976

Favourite opera

I have two – *Parsifal*, not only for itself but for the very special association it has for me, and *The Marriage of Figaro* by Mozart. *Parsifal* was the piece which I was already feeling very close to in my teens, and I used to play it through on Good Friday every year, and just try to evoke the atmosphere of Bayreuth's Festspielhaus where I first saw it in the 60s. And then of course in 1983, I worked with Reginald Goodall on it and when he became ill, I was asked to conduct the performances. Then it came up again 20 years later in 2003. *The Marriage of Figaro* is the piece I have conducted more than any other opera. These two wonderful pieces were linked for me in one of the most joyous weeks of my conducting career in September 2003. We were in Bristol and I conducted *Figaro* on the Tuesday and *Parsifal* on the Saturday.

Favourite memory

The most emotional moment was the feeling after I conducted my first *Don Giovanni*. I had waited until I was 50, and I had already done all the other Mozart operas. During the interval I was quite overwhelmed by the thought that I was conducting my first *Don Giovanni* – it was not so much while I was doing it, but once I was finished, it was just remarkable.

Wagner *Parsifal* 2003

About to conduct *Parsifal*, conductor Vladimir Jurowski wrote: 'I find that *Parsifal* needs a connector, a communicator, but not an interpreter. *Parsifal* to me is one of those exceptions in music, where nothing needs to be added: this universe needs to be just carefully carried to the people. I am also aware of the fact, that, as I am conducting my first *Parsifal*, I won't come even close to the solution of its problems, but since I hope that I will be privileged many other times to get in touch with this great work by conducting it, I am starting to see the resolution of these problems as a kind of lifetime goal, to which I could dedicate myself.'

Sara Fulgoni as Kundry, Robert Hayward as Amfortas, Alfred Reiter as Gurnemanz and Stephen O'Mara as Parsifal. Photograph Brian Tarr

Wagner *The Flying Dutchman* 2006

The Flying Dutchman saw for the
first time in a decade the return of
Bryn Terfel to WNO, the company
where he made his professional
debut. Conducted by Carlo Rizzi
and directed by David Pountney,
The Flying Dutchman also featured
video projection from two of the
UK's most acclaimed video artists,
Jane and Louise Wilson. *The Flying
Dutchman* (with Robert Hayward
taking over the title role) was
performed at the Grand Theatre
in Swansea on 15 April 2006 – 60
years to the day since WNO's first
performance in 1946.
Carlo Rizzi Conductor, with
Bryn Terfel as The Dutchman
Photograph Neil Bennett

Mussorgsky *Boris Godunov* 1988

Russian

WNO has found enormous success with operas from the Russian repertoire, including Tchaikovsky's *Eugene Onegin* and *The Queen of Spades*, and Mussorgsky's *Boris Godunov*. 2004 saw the launch of the WNO Russian Series, which will offer a number of major operatic works by Russian composers over a five year period, the first being James Macdonald's critically-acclaimed production of *Eugene Onegin*.

Carlo Rizzi said: 'For me *Boris Godunov* is an almost mystical opera, an opera in which every world has a feeling to express. It is one in which you find something unique that is related to the Russian people, Russian soul and Russian civilisation.

The emotional effect is extremely difficult to achieve, but what is sublime is that if you achieve it, it is a gift from God.'
Willard White as Boris Godunov
Photograph Clive Barda

Simon Cornish
Construction Manager, Cardiff Theatrical Services
With WNO since 1980

Favourite opera

It must be Tchaikovsky's *The Queen of Spades*. I have worked on three productions for different companies and WNO's in 2000 was superb. The music is great, but I just love the story. I find the characters very real and you can place this story smack bang in the present day. Herman is trying to find the secret of winning at cards, but in the end it's enough to put you off gambling forever.

Favourite production

It is Verdi's *Falstaff* directed by Peter Stein. The early 1980s were halcyon days for me when I was assistant to David Holland, then head of CTS and a good friend. Sadly David died in 1988, aged 34, from cancer. *Falstaff* was the last show that David and I worked on together and although it was hard work, it holds fond memories for me. I thought the production was great - I will always remember Donald Maxwell as Falstaff hiding in that wicker skip... great stuff! After David died, I decided to stay at CTS and continue the work that he had started. I became Construction Manager for CTS and have continued working for what is now a thriving part of WNO.

Tchaikovsky *The Queen of Spades* 2000

Tchaikovsky *Eugene Onegin* 2004

Tugan Sokhiev's first new production for WNO as Music Director was *Eugene Onegin*, directed by James Macdonald. This important production marked the first of WNO's Russian Series. In *The Times* Richard Morrison wrote: 'Knowing the vaguaries of the opera world, one hesitates to announce the dawn of a new golden era at Welsh National Opera. But if the other Tchaikovsky, Mussorgsky and Shostakovich pieces scheduled by its 26 year-old Music Director, Tugan Sokhiev are as fresh as this mesmerising *Onegin*, then WNO will soon be known as the best Russian opera company west of St Petersburg.'
Amanda Roocroft as Tatyana and Vladimir Moroz as Onegin
Photograph Bill Cooper

Léhar *The Merry Widow* 2005

Not forgetting...

Many of WNO's outstanding productions are not easy to group by award or by composer, but are no less important. Some are rarely seen, while others are the bread and butter of opera-goers. What binds them together is the exceptional talent, vision and world-class quality of Welsh National Opera.

For *The Merry Widow*, soprano Lesley Garrett returned to the stage after an absence of some years, and to WNO where she began her career. Singing the title role of Hanna Glawari, she said: 'I fell in love with Hanna years ago, but realised that I needed a certain amount of maturity to play her. I felt I needed a certain seniority because she's a commanding character. She's sure of herself and she organises her life the way she wants it to be. She takes risks, she's bold and she's not afraid to go where other women have never gone. I needed to experience those things myself before I could play that character.'

Lesley Garrett as Hanna Glawari
Photograph Bill Cooper

Berg *Wozzeck* 1986

In *The Observer* Nicholas Kenyon wrote: 'Berg's *Wozzeck* is one of the most powerfully and intricately organised of all operas. Liviu Ciulei's new production for WNO powerfully and intricately disorganises it. The precision of Berg's scheme is first peeled apart then reassembled in a fluid nightmarish sequence.

Ciulei has found such a strong visual and emotional framework for his statement that the result is compelling.'
Philip Joll as Wozzeck
Photograph Clive Barda

Wendy Franklin
Chorus, Auditions and Scheduling Manager
With WNO since 1972

Favourite production

It has to be between Michael Geliot's *Billy Budd*, which I think was a very true production and is completely unbeatable – it was a solid wooden ship, a cut-through showing all the decks which weighed tons – but I also adored Ciulei's *Wozzeck*. I like the whole way Berg writes, though I know *Wozzeck* is quite sinister. That production was wackier even than our recent Richard Jones production – all the sets were made out of giant copper springs which either hung down, or were curled into shapes on the floor, or dropped in and clipped to other bars to become the bunks for the soldiers. The backdrop was replaced in the last act by a paper one, and the crew were on scaffold behind it with watering cans. In the last bars of the opera, the crew just poured red paint down the paper like a sea of blood and it continued after the music had stopped. And after the red, came the black paint like annihilation over the blood. It never failed to get to the audience.

Favourite memory

Doing the full *Ring Cycle* on tour – not many people have done that; and also the foreign tours we have done, especially the first one to Switzerland – we took *Billy Budd* to Lausanne and Zurich. Not only was it the Company's first foreign tour but it was my first trip outside the UK too.

Stravinsky *The Rake's Progress* 1986

Coming shortly after the Millennium Commission turned down the application for Lottery funding for the Cardiff Bay Opera House, Matthew Warchus's production saw the last appearances for WNO by Bryn Terfel for ten years. In *The Daily Telegraph* Brian Hunt wrote: 'Bryn Terfel, Wales's brightest new star, has threatened that this may be his last appearance in his homeland if Cardiff does not get a new opera house.

His Shadow emphasises the potential loss. His massive presence and vocal domination make him ideal for the role, icily feigning servitude to his master, Tom, when the polarity is in reality reversed.'

Bryn Terfel as Nick Shadow,
Paul Nilon as Tom Rakewell and
Alwyn Mellor as Anne
Photograph Robbie Jack above
Photograph Clive Barda right

Matthew Epstein
General Director
With WNO from 1991 to 1994

Favourite opera

This is too tough really – I suppose Berlioz's *Les Troyens* comes to mind, but then perhaps it should be *The Marriage of Figaro* which has been a throughline throughout my life from when I first listened to it as a teenager. Over the years I have seen or worked with some great casts and great productions of *Figaro*, and the highlights have definitely been because of the outstanding productions.

Favourite production

I think it has to be *Pelléas and Mélisande* – this was a masterpiece production planned by Brian McMaster before he left, but I had the joy of working on it with Peter Stein and Pierre Boulez, and the superb cast. It was a huge undertaking, probably the biggest production the company had ever done. It was really too big for the New Theatre first time round, though everyone enjoyed it. We finally really got it right in the revival in 1994 which opened in Birmingham. Everything was right technically and running smoothly, and of course we also took it to Le Châtelet in Paris too, which was quite exceptional. Of the other productions which I worked on, *Beatrice and Benedict* also has to be a favourite and also *Cendrillon* directed by Robert Carson was fantastic.

Berlioz *The Trojans* 1987

The Trojans was created together with Scottish Opera and Opera North, and sponsored by IBM. WNO was the first of the companies to perform the whole work, and that evening was the first conducted by Charles Mackerras as WNO's new Music Director. In *The Daily Telegraph* Robert Henderson wrote: 'As much to singers, producer and designer, it is to Sir Charles Mackerras that the performance owed its brilliance and grandeur, the thrust and energy of his conducting shaping the music in huge sweeping curves.'
Anne Evans as Cassandra and Philip Joll as Chorebus
Photograph Catherine Ashmore

Berlioz's final opera was based on *Much Ado about Nothing*, and Elijah Moshinsky was determined to retain the humour of Shakespeare's play. Conductor John Nelson said: 'If you want something that is lovely, and joyful, and puts a smile on everybody's face, this is it. This piece is a tonic. We're having fun, and that's not a bad emotion to have in this dark world of ours.'

Rebecca Evans as Hero and Karl Morgan Daymond as Claudio
Photograph Bill Cooper

Berlioz *Beatrice and Benedict* 1994

Sara Evans
Development Manager
With WNO since 1985

Favourite opera

I find it impossible to choose between two operas. *Così fan tutte* is Mozart at his very best - fantastic solo arias, heart-breakingly beautiful ensembles, exquisite orchestration – from the very first note of the overture, one is mesmerised. I also love Tchaikovsky's *Eugene Onegin*. I just love the Russian-ness of this piece - gorgeous lyrical lines, rich harmonies, wonderful dances. The story is also a great favourite of mine, having read the Pushkin original at an impressionable age – so romantic and so sad!

Favourite production

The one that has stuck in my mind is Peter Stein's production of Verdi's *Falstaff*. I had a great time with that production – a full tour of England and Wales managing enormous parties twice a week for the sponsor, NatWest. The cast included such names as Laurence Dale, Paul Charles Clarke and Wendy Verco, with Richard Armstrong conducting. All the cast were marvellous - Donald Maxwell, Suzanne Murphy, Nuccia Focile and the others. They came to as many sponsor's receptions as they could manage. And then it toured to New York, Milan and Tokyo – what a production!

Maxwell Davies *The Doctor of Myddfai* 1996

WNO commissioned Sir Peter Maxwell Davies to write an opera to celebrate its 50th anniversary in 1996. The libretto, which included Welsh-language songs, was written by David Pountney, who also directed, and was based on a 12th century Welsh folk tale. The world première was on 10 July 1996 at the North Wales Theatre in Llandudno, following preview performances in Cardiff. Photograph Bill Cooper

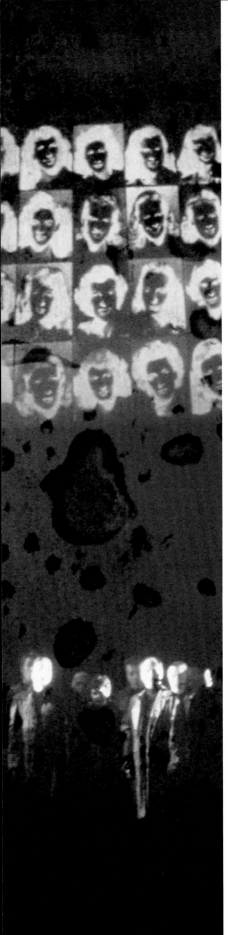

Ian Siddall
Scenic Art Manager, Cardiff Theatrical Services
With WNO since 1978

Favourite production

For technical reasons alone my favourite WNO opera was Peter Maxwell Davies's *The Doctor of Myddfai*, which was commissioned by WNO. Sue Huntley and Donna Muir were the designers and their approach was really groundbreaking with plenty of technically difficult artistic problems. No area of the stage was left unused - there was even action in the top left hand corner of the proscenium arch as singers were raised up on a platform and lit behind a gauze with large rain drops painted on it. There was a creative buzz in the place and a great mixture of humour and creativity and the whole team felt part of the creative process. As always when this happens people raised their game to even higher levels than normal and I left the theatre after the dress rehearsal feeling that I had worked on something really special.

Mascagni *Cavalleria rusticana* 1996

Anne-Marie Owens as Santuzza
Photograph Bill Cooper

Leoncavallo *Pagliacci* 1996

The double-bill of *Cavalleria rusticana* and *Pagliacci* was WNO's first ever production, performed on 15 April 1946. Elijah Moshinsky's new production premièred as part of WNO's 50th birthday celebrations on 15 April 1996, and also formed part of WNO's opening season in its new home in Wales Millennium Centre in 2005.

Dennis O'Neill as Canio
2003 revival
Photographer Bill Cooper

In *The Guardian* Rian Evans wrote
about the revival of the production
of *Salome* by André Engels in 2002
'To say that one left the theatre with
a feeling of nausea is not the most
obvious recommendation for an
opera, but when the work in question
is Strauss's *Salome*, it is never going
to be a salutary experience. It is not
so much the gory sight of the head
of John the Baptist – Jokanaan – on
a platter that creates this effect so
much as the insidious way in which
Strauss builds up atmosphere.
The score has the pacing of a modern
psychological thriller. Conductor
Carlo Rizzi's reading for WNO creates
a gradual but insistent onslaught on
the senses, Salome's music becoming
as beautiful as she is depraved.'
Stephanie Sundine as Salome
Photograph Catherine Ashmore

Strauss *Salome* 1988

Sir Brian McMaster
With WNO from 1976 to 1991

Favourite opera
Wagner's *Die Meistersinger von Nürnberg* because it's about a whole world and just about everything that affects a human being, which is ultimately what I think theatre should be. And of course opera is theatre.

Favourite production
I don't have a favourite, I really don't – so many of them I loved working on and seeing.

Best memory
Joining WNO.

Worst memory
Leaving WNO.

Director Calixto Bieito said:
'The music of *Die Fledermaus* is
superficially happy, but it is a
happiness that conceals a hypocrisy.
The root of this hypocrisy is a society
that creates and applies strict rules
about personal conduct that exist
in parallel with licentiousness.
The atmosphere of this production
is of an eternal party. It goes on
everlastingly, round the clock, in the
same location. It is a kind of hell.
At this perpetual party, various games
are played. In this case, the game is
the game of prison, a kind of mental
prison. On another day, the game
might be a different one.
Guests arrive and leave, but the
party goes on.'

Photograph Clive Barda

Strauss *Die Fledermaus* 2002

Ariadne auf Naxos marked the return of Carlo Rizzi to WNO as Music Director. In *The Sunday Times* Hugh Canning wrote: 'At the first night of *Ariadne* in Cardiff's New Theatre, the audience welcomed Rizzi back like the prodigal son and he treated them to a beautifully conducted account of this gorgeous score: the wind soloists sounded world class in the rewarding music Strauss wrote for them and were clearly overjoyed to have Rizzi back.' D'Arcy Bleiker as Harlequin and Katarzyna Dondalska as Zerbinetta Photograph Clive Barda

Strauss *Ariadne auf Naxos* 2004

Marilyn Stolz
Board Administrator/HR Manager
With WNO since 1975

Favourite opera

For the heart-rending passion of the music it's Puccini's *Manon Lescaut*. It was the first opera I ever saw back in 1975 when I joined WNO and it converted me to opera on the spot. I felt like I had died with them at the end but really something had been born in me – a love of opera that has enriched my life for the past thirty years. But for the atmosphere and the almost tangible sound and feel of the sea, I also love Britten's *Billy Budd*.

Best memory

The year that our scenery store burned down in the late 1970s. As disasters go the timing could not have been worse – we were about to go into the New Theatre and all our sets went up in flames. But what makes it my best memory is the fact that the opera community came to our rescue in a most spectacular way. We put on the season using sets kindly loaned to us at no cost by the other opera houses. Luckily our costumes were stored elsewhere so they survived, but it was all hands to the wheel and I clearly remember learning the art of 'scrimming' as I helped the Props Department rebuild statues that were lost in the fire. It was an emotional time and it was wonderful to see everyone pulling together in our hour of need.

WNO MAX

WNO MAX was conceived and created in 2001 out of a radical ambition: that WNO and the community it serves should develop side by side, as equal partners in an adventurous programme of work that draws on and inspires the creativity of all its participants. It aims to bring out the operatic in everyone, across a range of ages, communities and abilities.

WNO MAX commissioned this oratorio for 500 community singers, the WNO Orchestra, and soloists from the Wales Millennium Centre Chorus. Inspired by a Gabriel García Márquez story, the oratorio explores the regeneration of a community through creativity, and as such celebrated the newly opened Wales Millennium Centre. The project involved collaboration between WNO, Wales Millennium Centre and the resident companies. Orlando Gough and Richard Chew composed a multi-stylistic score that explodes the boundaries of choral singing.

The libretto was written by Gwyneth Lewis, National Poet of Wales, and captures the shifting atmosphere of an intriguing seashore encounter. Iain Paterson as The Beautiful Man Photograph Brian Tarr

WNO Education
The Cinderella Project 1993

In the years before WNO MAX, WNO had developed a vibrant education programme. One of its most ambitious projects, linking community and main stage operas, was *The Cinderella Project*. In the autumn of 1993, WNO put on four different versions of the fairytale Cinderella. WNO gave Massenet's *Cendrillon* its UK première on the main stage with Rebecca Evans in the title role. Meanwhile the more familiar *La Cenerentola* by Rossini was toured around leisure centres and small theatres in a score adapted for seven players. At Blackwood Miners' Institute, WNO brought together more than one hundred young singers to perform Peter Maxwell Davies's children's opera Cinderella, with costumes by fashion house Red or Dead; and in the Splott district of Cardiff, a new community musical was created – *The Splott Cinderella*.

Left: Peter Maxwell Davies's Cinderella
Below: Rebecca Evans in Cendrillon
Photograph Clive Barda

WNO MAX *Wise Eye* and *Through Listening Eyes*

Wise Eye

Wise Eye is a chamber opera for baritone, children's chorus, piano and violin. WNO MAX commissioned it in 2001 for participation and performance by young people in special schools. It was written and composed by Richard Chew in response to Janáček's *The Cunning Little Vixen*. *Wise Eye* follows the life of a young fox, and has involved children from across Wales and England.

Through Listening Eyes

Through Listening Eyes is an extraordinary collaboration between Welsh National Opera and Touch Trust. This short film, made by Richard Aylwin, captures the engagement with opera and with each other, of artists, musicians and a remarkable group of young people and adults with profound intellectual and multiple disabilities. It explores the opera *Wise Eye*, and is an intimate witness to creativity.
Images Richard Aylwin

In 2003 WNO MAX took over Brunel's Passenger Shed at Bristol Temple Meads Station for *Opera in the Shed* - a festival of workshops, demonstrations and performances. At its heart was *City Songs*, a song cycle written by 200 Bristol primary school children in tribute to their city, performed with the WNO Orchestra. The children worked with composer Karen Wimhurst and poet Clare Williamson, exploring Bristol, their sense of citizenship and their aspirations for the future. In 2004, *City Songs* was recreated by children who reworked the story and songs to reflect their home city of Cardiff. Photograph Brian Tarr

WNO MAX *City Songs* 2003

WNO MAX *Chorus!* 2004

WNO MAX conceived *Chorus!* as a way of celebrating the fantastic and-wide-ranging performance skills of the WNO Chorus, and to encourage new audiences into the opera. This production, directed by David Pountney, toured to WNO's main UK theatres and featured a wide and exciting combination of opera choruses. *Chorus!* was accompanied by the WNO Orchestra, conducted by the WNO Chorus Master, Donald Nally.
Photograph Brian Tarr

WNO MAX *Redflight Barcud* 2005

WNO MAX has commissioned a trilogy of bilingual chamber operas, the *Land Sea Sky Trilogy*, for community audiences in rural Wales. The operas highlight conservation issues, and involve young people from each community in the performances. The Sky opera, *Redflight Barcud* follows a family of endangered red kites. Gwyneth Lewis wrote the libretto, and Richard Chew composed the opera. *Redflight Barcud* premièred in a marquee in the village of Cilycwm in Carmarthenshire, which is at the heart of work to preserve the red kite population. The Sea opera, *Dolffin*, opened in March 2006 in Cardigan Bay, and the Land opera, *Wild Cat*, exploring the mysterious cats of North Wales opens in spring 2007.

Mark Evans as Father Kite,
Craig Yates as Teenage Kite
Ros Evans as Girl Kite
Photograph Kirsten McTernan

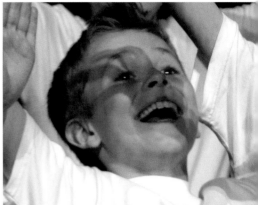

WNYO *The Tailor's Daughter* 2005

Youth Opera

Welsh National Youth Opera is South Wales based group of young performers aged 14–25 who are wildly enthusiastic about opera. They develop skills in workshops throughout the year and create annual performances with WNO artists. The WNO Singing Club is for young singers aged 10–13 who have experienced a WNO MAX project in school. Members of this group meet weekly to develop their skills and love for singing.

Jenny Walker as The Tailor's Daughter and
David Thaxton as The Wolf
Photograph Brian Tarr

WNYO *The Tailor's Daughter* 2005

In collaboration with the Arts Council of Northern Ireland and the Belfast Grand Opera House, WNO MAX commissioned a new opera, *The Tailor's Daughter*, especially for the Youth Opera Group. Belfast-based Brian Irvine composed the music, and Welsh writer Greg Cullen wrote the libretto. *The Tailor's Daughter* is a fairytale to appeal particularly to young and family audiences, and its world première in April 2005 in the Weston Studio of WMC received great acclaim.

Photograph Brian Tarr

Verdi *Don Carlos* 2005

Supported by the Friends of WNO and the WNO Don Carlos Syndicate
By 2007, The Friends of WNO have supported 14 productions since 1983 and are set to raise an accumulated £1 million by 2007. WNO has created a new approach to fundraising, with the introduction of syndicates of individuals with an interest in supporting particular operas or composers, so far comprising syndicates for *Don Carlos* and *The Flying Dutchman*.
The Chorus of WNO
Photograph Bill Cooper

Today WNO is...

It started as a group of amateurs rehearsing in a car showroom. Sixty years on, Welsh National Opera is an internationally-renowned company. But how many of its audiences know much more about WNO than what they see on the stage?

Caroline Leech offers a snapshot of WNO at 60 as it reaches audiences across the UK in theatres, schools, community halls and even in tents. Who does it perform to, who supports it and how far does its influence reach?

Today Welsh National Opera is...
one of the most highly regarded
opera companies in Europe. It tours
extensively each year throughout the
UK, making it not only the national
opera company of Wales, but also the
largest provider of opera to regional
England. The Company had an annual
residency in Belfast for a number of
years, and 2005 saw WNO's first visit
to the Edinburgh Festival Theatre.

WNO has a permanent company
of over 250 people, comprising
the Orchestra and Chorus, and
music, production, technical and
administrative staff. Every season
the Company also welcomes guest
singers, conductors, directors and
designers, who enjoy international
careers and work in major opera
houses across the world.

WNO's work and audiences
For many years, WNO has produced
nine full-scale operas in three
seasons - spring, summer and

autumn. Each season has on average
one new production and two revivals.
From the 2006/7 season, WNO will
perform full UK tours in the autumn
and spring seasons, culminating in
an annual summer 'festival season'
with performances in Cardiff and
Birmingham.

WNO MAX
At the heart of the Company
is WNO MAX. Unique to WNO,
WNO MAX aims to maximise the
Company's resources with a diverse
and integrated programme of
performances, projects and education
initiatives beyond the main stage.
This programme creates new
opportunities for the WNO ensemble
and for the communities it reaches,
maximising the potential of opera
to electrify and enrapture, through
participation in and preparation for
live opera experiences. In 2005/6
WNO MAX reached an audience of
over 31,000 people.

WNO MAX commissions artists
to make new work, and invites
experienced WNO performers to
take on new artistic challenges by
performing the work that results.

In a WNO MAX project, the energy
and creativity of the community
comes together with WNO's
outstanding musical and theatrical
forces to provide a brilliant evening
at the opera for everyone. This does
not mean doorstep deliveries of
classic repertoire – it means making
new operas to engage specific
audiences. Through the work of WNO
MAX, the Company work with opera
in ways that transform people's sense
both of the artform itself and of their
own creative potential.

WNO's new work
WNO is strongly committed to
the continuing development of
opera as an artform through the
commissioning of new work. The
WNO MAX programme commissions

new opera and music theatre from some of the UK's most exciting composers, writers, poets, artists and film-makers.

On the main stage in 2007, WNO will give the world première of an opera it has commissioned from James MacMillan, one of the most important composers of his generation. *The Sacrifice* will be a drama of politics and passion. It will open at Wales Millennium Centre in autumn 2007 and will tour across the UK.

The WNO Company

In addition to its operatic work, the award-winning Chorus and Orchestra of Welsh National Opera undertake a number of non-operatic engagements each year. The Orchestra plays a series of orchestral concerts at St David's Hall in Cardiff, as well as its annual Tour of Wales, which travels to leisure centres and town halls in the more rural areas of

Wales that cannot support the full operatic company. In addition to its small-scale touring and concert hall appearances, the Chorus of WNO have sung at prestigious events such as Her Majesty The Queen's opening of the National Assembly for Wales and at the Millennium Stadium.

WNO is proud of its development of young professionals across all its disciplines – not only singers, but also musical, administrative and technical professions. Many of the best singers, directors and conductors of Wales and the UK have began their careers with WNO. The WNO Associate Artists Programme offers young principal singers the chance to learn roles and work with WNO music staff while performing roles in main operas. WNO's continued involvement in BBC Cardiff Singer of the World where the Orchestra of WNO is one of two resident orchestras, also brings many young singers to WNO from across the world.

Wales Millennium Centre
Photograph Peter Gill

Donald Gordon Theatre, WMC
Photograph Chris Colclough

Glanfa Foyer, WMC
Photograph Kiran Ridley

Berg *Wozzeck* 2005
Supported by the Garfield Weston
Foundation and the WNO Partnership
The Garfield Weston Foundation has
supported WNO with very generous
gifts towards core funding, securing
a number of WNO MAX projects,

as well as many main stage operas.
The WNO Partnership is made up of
individuals giving philanthropically
and has supported ten productions in
ten years, all of which are from the
more challenging repertoire.

Peter Hoare as The Captain,
Christopher Purves as Wozzeck and
Clive Bayley as The Doctor
Photograph Bill Cooper

WNO's reputation for high quality productions is borne out by the number of co-productions it undertakes with opera companies all over Europe, the USA and Australia each year. Co-productions allow companies not only to share the cost of creating an opera production, for example in terms of designs and sets, but it also allows a cross-fertilisation of artistic ideas across the world.

WNO at WMC

In February 2005, WNO opened its first season in its new home in the outstanding new Wales Millennium Centre (WMC), built on reclaimed dockland in Cardiff Bay. Sitting as it does next to the new home of the National Assembly for Wales, the development of WMC lay at the heart of the regeneration of the Bay area.

WMC is one of the most exciting cultural buildings to have been created in Europe in decades. WNO's needs, artistically and technically, were integral to the design of the new building, and its acoustics were designed to be perfect for opera. Not only is it home to Welsh National Opera and six other diverse arts organisations, but is also an international presenting house for ballet, dance and large-scale musicals.

After 59 years of working across a number of sites in Cardiff, WMC has enabled WNO to bring its rehearsal, administrative and performing base into one building for the first time. WNO's set-building and props workshops are housed only five minutes drive from WMC.

From 1954 to 2004, WNO gave its Cardiff performances in the New Theatre, which seats just over 1,000 people for opera. The Donald Gordon Theatre in WMC houses 1,750 for WNO performances. This additional 750 seats for each performance in WMC allowed WNO to drive forward a ground-breaking pricing strategy which has proved enormously successful, and which has been fêted by politicians and critics alike. From its first season in February 2005, WNO dropped its seat prices dramatically, with 250 tickets available for every performance for just £5. The excitement with which this announcement was met, along with WNO's new subscription package, meant that WNO's early seasons in WMC sold out well in advance.

Research showed that the £5 tickets attracted many new people to opera, and in general the pricing strategy encouraged seasoned opera-goers to attend a more diverse range of operas than they might have done in the past.

The more modern and larger facilities have now allowed WNO to use the enormous benefits in size, space and equipment in its new home, to create more artistically and technically challenging operas to bring to all its audiences across the UK.

WNO's funding

To achieve its current level and range of activity, WNO relies not only on the income it earns at the box office, but on the unique combination of the public funding it receives from the taxpayer and, increasingly, from the private sector. A crucial partnership exists between public funding via the Arts Council of Wales and Arts Council England, and that contributed by individual donors, patrons, business sponsors, trusts and foundations. Taken on their own, the Arts Council grants are insufficient to sustain WNO, but when brought together and combined with the contributions of private supporters, the result is a vibrant, developing company offering exceptional value to audiences and communities in England and Wales.

Earned income
WNO sets itself challenging targets for income earned at the box office each year for its main opera seasons, as well as its other work. In 2005/6, the Company raised almost £3 million at the box office towards its running costs and future productions.

Public funding

In 2005/6, WNO's annual revenue funding from the Arts Council of Wales was £4.25 million and from Arts Council England was £5.9 million.

In February 2002, the Arts Councils of Wales and England announced they would support a five-year strategic plan created by WNO as a result of a two-year self-analysis under the Stabilisation Programme. The creation and implementation of the plan, led by Executive Director Peter Bellingham, has enabled the Company to re-focus its mainscale touring in England and Wales, and substantially increase its investment in community and education work. During the life of the plan, WNO was also able to access up to £4.25 million of National Lottery funding over five years.

Private support and sponsorship

WNO is supported by a significant number of people and organisations who contribute money, and sometimes services, to the Company for its work. These contributions have increased and become ever more important to the Company since the early 1990s, and the main sources include individual donors (who also leave legacies), trusts, foundations and corporate sponsors. The sums raised annually are now in excess of £1.5 million (or 10% of turnover) and are set to grow towards £2 million by 2010.

Securing support from the audiences and individuals who value WNO is a key development goal for the Company today. The Friends of WNO have been contributing and fundraising since the 1980s and are set to have raised an accumulated £1 million by 2007 when they will sponsor their 15th production since 1983. Supporting a new production each season, The WNO Partnership of regular donors was established during the 50th Anniversary season in 1995/96. Ten years and ten important productions later, including *The Queen of Spades*, *Katya Kabanova* and *Jephtha*, the WNO Partnership too has contributed more than £1 million to WNO.

New initiatives to attract major gifts and legacies, small syndicates of support, and regular giving from a wide audience appeal are all currently under way to develop individual giving as the most reliable source of private funding for the Company into the future.

WNO enjoys a particular reputation for attracting and retaining corporate sponsors and was one of the first organisations in Britain to attract business support when National Westminster Bank sponsored a series of new productions during the 1980s,

Verdi *La traviata* 2004
Sponsored by Coutts & Co
Coutts & Co is WNO's largest corporate sponsor and has sponsored seven productions and seasons, over the last seven years, including *Hansel and Gretel*, *La traviata* and *The Flying Dutchman*.
Nuccia Focile as Violetta
Photograph Clive Barda

Redflight Barcud 2005
Sponsored by ScottishPower
A long succession of north Wales seasons and more recently significant WNO MAX projects have been supported by ScottishPower and before that Manweb over the last eight years.
Mark Evans as Father Kite
Photograph Kirsten McTernan

while the US oil company Amoco funded WNO's London seasons from the late 1970s for more than 20 years.

Today it is Coutts & Co who enjoy the major association with WNO's performances around the UK, having sponsored seven productions and tours in the last seven years, as well as a regular series of recitals in London, elsewhere in England and internationally. Associated British Ports is in its 19th year of sponsorship and is firmly linked to WNO's move to Wales Millennium Centre, to the Company's spring seasons and to special projects there. ScottishPower (formerly Manweb) secures WNO's presence in north Wales and has been a critical partner, sponsoring and supporting the development of WNO MAX over the last eight years.

Arts and education trusts and foundations are very prominent in the mix of contributors, with the Garfield Weston Foundation providing the most significant core funding to ensure WNO's survival and development during the last 12 years.

WNO's media
WNO's work has been broadcast regularly on radio and television in the UK. It has a unique relationship with S4C, the Welsh-language channel, which has televised eight WNO productions since 1996. The BBC has regularly broadcast WNO's operas on BBC Radio 3, as well as on television on BBC2 and BBC4. WNO is a Classic FM Partner and works closely with its presenters to help newcomers make their first foray into live opera.

Cardiff Theatrical Services
In 1984, WNO's workshops became Cardiff Theatrical Services, a wholly owned subsidiary of WNO, which is now one of the UK's leading set-building companies for opera and theatre. Based in a workshop on the Tyndall Street Estate in Cardiff, CTS offers a complete manufacturing service, including carpentry, joinery, engineering, metal fabrication, painting, sculpting and specialist cloth sewing.

As well as undertaking the building of all WNO's new productions and refurbishment of existing sets, CTS has developed an international reputation, working with clients such as The Royal Opera House, Glyndebourne Opera, English National Opera, and Opera North, as well as the Royal National Theatre, Royal Shakespeare Company, Lyric Opera Chicago, Monte Carlo Opera and La Scala, Milan. CTS has also supplied sets for musicals such as *Joseph and his Technicolour Dreamcoat* in the West End, and in 2005 built a double-barrelled revolving stage for the beautiful new Tenerife Opera House. For television, the interior set for the new time-travelling TARDIS was also built by CTS for BBC Wales's recreation of *Doctor Who* in 2004.

Cardiff Theatrical Services
Photographs Brian Tarr

184

Sponsored by Associated British Ports
Associated British Ports has been
integral to the redevelopment of
the Cardiff Bay area and to securing
a home for WNO. ABP is WNO's
longest-standing sponsor, after
19 years of unbroken support.
Photograph Brian Tarr

The Most Beautiful Man from the Sea 2005

The Editor's thanks

Opera brings together many artforms – music, literature, drama, visual arts, dance and, in certain productions, film – in one glorious live spectacle.

This book offers a tribute to the many directors, designers, singers, musicians, dancers, actors, technicians and craftspeople who have given so much talent, skill and vision to Welsh National Opera, in particular over the last 20 years.

There is, however, another group of talented artists in opera - the production photographers.

Their skill lies in being able to capture all the essential ingredients of a live opera in still-life, and in balancing the artistic imperative with the practical. WNO has commissioned some of the UK's best theatre production photographers over the last 20 years or more, and this book is witness to their art.

My thanks and enormous respect goes to them - in particular to Bill Cooper, Clive Barda, Catherine Ashmore and Brian Tarr, who have been the artists behind most of WNO's photographic archive since 1985. Brian, especially, has not only photographed productions, but also many rehearsals, portraits and other events each year.

My thanks also go to the other contributors: Richard Fawkes and to Simon Rees, whose knowledge of the Company between them is immense; and to Neil Bennett and Kiran Ridley, whose endless patience, sensitivity and good humour allowed them into places where cameras are seldom welcomed. Their pictures are all the more delightful because of that.

On a personal note my thanks go to Anthony Freud, Carlo Rizzi, Lucy Shorrocks, Lucy Stout, Hazel Hardy, Catriona Chatterley, and many other people at WNO for all their help and support throughout the development of this book; and of course, my love and thanks go to Perryn Leech, WNO's Technical Director.

Thanks too to everyone at Graffeg, and in particular to Kelly Walters, Carwyn Lloyd Jones and of course Peter Gill, for their guidance and patience, and for their beautiful design and production.

The Company of Welsh National Opera is an exceptionally talented family of artists, technicians, craftspeople and administrators. Together they will undoubtedly make the next 60 years even better than the last.

Caroline Leech

For more information

If you would like more information about WNO and its work, contact:

WNO Marketing on 0800 328 2357 or marketing@wno.org.uk

or visit the WNO website on www.wno.org.uk

On the website you can see the full WNO diary, cast lists, production and theatre information, plot summaries, reviews and audio highlights from each opera.

WNO has also created a website - www.fresh2opera.co.uk - developed especially for people who are new to opera.

Photographers
www.briantarr.co.uk
www.kiranridley.com
www.neilbennettphotography.com
office@catherineashmore.co.uk
www.clivebarda.com
bill-cooper@btconnect.com

The contributors

Richard Fawkes

Richard Fawkes is an award-winning writer and director. The author of nine books (including *Welsh National Opera*, published in 1986), he has also written for TV, radio and the stage, and the librettos for *Survival Song* (nominated for an Olivier Award) and *Biko*, both with music by Priti Paintal. His directing credits include the award-winning Channel 4 series *Tom Keating on Painters* and *The Original Three Tenors* (about Caruso, Gigli and Bjorling). Stage direction includes *The Yeomen of the Guard* for Opera Holland Park and *Faust* for Opera South. His favourite opera is *Der Rosenkavalier*.

Simon Rees

Simon Rees is Dramaturg of Welsh National Opera, where he has worked since 1989, editing programmes, researching productions, giving talks and translating libretti. After studying English at Cambridge he taught in Italy and at Kyoto University, Japan. He has published translations, reviews and three novels: *The Devil's Looking-Glass, Making a Snowman* and *Nathaniel and Mrs Palmer* (winning a Trask Award and a Hawthornden Fellowship). He has translated more than 60 opera librettos for surtitles, and has made singing translations for a number of opera companies and festivals. He has also worked on the BBC Cardiff

Singer of the World competition since 1989, and scripted the six-part documentary *Soul of a Nation* for BBC2 Wales. He lives in Cardiff. His favourite opera is *The Marriage of Figaro*.

Brian Tarr

Brian Tarr is a photographer from Cardiff. He has been working for WNO since 1981 as a production photographer as well as taking technical and company portraits. Brian took all the mugshot portraits which formed the backdrop to Christopher Alden's *Turandot* in 1994. He specialises in theatrical photography and has worked with many companies across Wales. His favourite opera is Verdi's *Otello*, particularly the WNO production by Peter Stein.

Kiran Ridley

Kiran Ridley is a dynamic young award-winning photographer currently working in the UK. Achievements to date include finalist in the Association of Photographers 'Document' Awards in 2005; Highly Commended in the Ian Parry Award; finalist for 'Young Photographer of the Year' in the 2003 'Picture Editor's Awards; finalist in The Observer Hodge Award, and The Tom Webster Award 1998. Kiran has exhibited in several venues including Exposure at the Royal Photographic Society, the

Tom Blau Gallery, London and at Ffotogallery & CBAT Gallery, Cardiff. His work has been published in *The Sunday Times Magazine*, *The Times* and *The Financial Times*, *The Washington Post*, *The Independent on Saturday Magazine*, *The Independent*, he *Guardian Magazine*, *Observer* and *Guardian newspapers*, and in *The Economist Magazine*. His favourite opera is *La traviata*.

Neil Bennett

Neil Bennett is an award-winning freelance photographer based in south Wales. His career began at the *Western Mail and Echo* in 1990, and over the past 16 years he has worked for various newspapers in Wales, Scotland and the US. He has covered a variety of subjects, from the Royal family to major sporting fixtures, as well as portraiture for magazine covers and arts events. His reportage assignments have taken him on projects in Africa - including famine in Ethiopia and Aids in Uganda - to New York in 2001. Neil now works from Cardiff for various clients, from *The Independent* and *The Observer* newspapers to BBC Wales and S4C, in addition to his own projects. His favourite opera is *Madam Butterfly*.

Index